How to Promote Your Children's Book

Second Edition, Revised and Expanded

How to Promote Your Children's Book

A Survival Guide for Published Writers

Second Edition, Revised and Expanded

Evelyn Gallardo

Evelyn Gallardo

Primate Productions

Published by
Primate Productions
P.O. Box 3038
Manhattan Beach, CA 90266
© 2000 by Evelyn Gallardo

First Edition published 1997
Second Edition published 2000, Revised
Printed in the United States of America

ISBN: 0-9665758-1-4

Printed in United States of America
by
Morris Publishing
3212 East Highway 30
Kearney, NE 68847
1-800-650-7888

For Janet, April, Robin, Joan G., Michelle, Alexis, Mary Ann, Joan P., Jeri, and Catherine
—Who are always there when I need a group hug.

—E.G.

Acknowledgments

My deep appreciation goes to Rachel Ballon for her inspiration and insight, and for holding my feet to the writing fire when I need her most. It was her wonderful idea to make this second edition interactive. Thanks also to my editor, Beverly Trainer, for putting my manuscript on her fast track. And finally, I'd like to thank Ane Miller, Shirley Russell, Judy Nelson, Dennis and Linda Ronberg, Susan Patron, Bonnie O'Brian, Brad Rumble, and the many other children's booksellers, librarians and teachers who embrace books, the kids who read them, and the authors who write them.

Table of Contents

Phase 1

Field Prep

Introduction

It's Still a Jungle Out There

You're amazing! You've performed a minor miracle. At times it was exciting, frightening, lonely, painful. In dark moments you wondered if your manuscript would ever see the light of day. But you saw it through. You wrote a book and it's been published. If this is your first literary venture you probably think promotion is your publisher's job. Well, wake up and smell the swamp because I'm about to deliver disappointing news. Unless you're a celebrity, your publisher's promotion budget will go to authors with proven track records and a series of titles. Precisely the authors who need it the least. But from the publisher's point of view, it makes perfect economic sense. They've already invested a hefty sum in you—a cub that's still wet behind the ears. It's a jungle out there. There's no use whimpering over it. The fact is you're untried and untested.

But here's the good news. If you approach book promotion as an exciting, creative adventure, you can be a king or queen of the jungle, and I'm going to show you how to do it. As a former Sales Promotions Manager for an international firm, I know what it takes to sell a product, and I'm willing to do it. I've applied the same skills and techniques to my own children's book, *Among the Orangutans*. It's gone into a second printing and a third. One day I got a call from my publisher asking for advice on the fourth printing. Would I be booking as many events the following year as the last? "More," was my answer and fourth printing was ordered. Friends began coming to me for advice and before long I was taking on clients. It was in response to their requests that I began jotting down notes for the first edition of *How to Promote Your Children's Book—A Survival Guide*.

As it turned out, writers were starved for this type of information and nitty-gritty guidance. The book was a best seller at the 1997 Society of Children's Book Writers & Illustrators (SCBWI) National Conference. Writers called, e-mailed and stopped me at conferences to express how much the book had helped them. Order inquiries continued long after the first printing had sold out. We've entered a new millennium and now, more than ever, writers like you are willing to step out from behind your computers, take the lion by the mane, and generate your own book signings, school and library visits, and conference events. You are experiencing the power and satisfaction that come with being in control. You are connecting with your audience in rewarding ways you never imagined. If you're a new reader exploring paths to promote your book, you came to the right place. If you've already read the first edition, welcome back. The difference in this second edition is that it is interactive. You're no longer a passive bystander. You not only learn how to accomplish a task, you see a real-life example of how I did it, then you create your own version right on the page. I've also added two new chapters, "Beat Your Tom-Tom—Create Promotion Material with Pizzazz," and "Around the World in 80 Seconds—Going Global on the Internet." Both chapters are designed to help you save money by utilizing new technologies.

It took time and talent to write your book, perseverance to get it published, and now, you've taken the courageous leap to learn how to promote it. You're already ten steps ahead of the herd. Through your efforts your book will enjoy future printings and your publisher will love you. So, cut loose with your best Tarzan yell, "Ah-ah-ah, ah-ah-ah!" and swing through the promotion canopy with confidence. This book is your compass. Let the adventure begin.

Chapter One

Survival Gear
Promotion Tools A-Z

To survive in the wild you need some essential tools—a compass, flashlight, matches, Swiss army knife, mosquito repellent, etc. If you want to explore media, bookseller, conference, school, library, and Internet habitats, you'll need to prepare and sharpen your professional-author tools. This is a comprehensive list, from which you can pick and choose. It defines each tool and explains how to create it. Examples and additional information are contained in related chapters. Continue to refer to this list as you become more experienced, then develop and use the tools that best fit your needs.

Autograph Pen - Sharpie Extra Fine Point and Pentel Fine Point pens dry fast on glossy paper. Buy them by the box and carry at least three to every event because the points do wear down. Ballpoint pens tend to smear on glossy paper but work well on soft-cover books.

Bio - A bio should read more like a literary piece than a résumé, for it's the centerpiece of your press kit. When you call program directors about speaking at conferences and other events, they may ask you to fax your bio. It can range from 1-3 pages, with 1 page being the preferred length. Like a good compass, an effective bio will lead the reader directly to a predetermined destination, whether it's a feature story about you or a speaking engagement. Your lead paragraph will feature your prominent accomplishments as they relate to your book. If you've written a biography, you'll mention your experience as a history teacher, but there's no need to carry on about your stint as a lab technician. The body of the bio includes recent achievements and awards, highlights in your life, education and any other interesting bits of information pertaining to your book. Conclude with an uplifting paragraph that looks to the future. See sample in Chapter Three.

Bookmark - Bookmarks can easily be designed on your computer. You can fit from 4-10 on a page, depending on the type size. Include your name, the title of your book, the publisher and the ISBN number. Consider adding the scanned cover of your book to catch the reader's eye. Copy the master onto card stock, and then cut. For a more festive look, punch a hole near the top and tie a short length of yarn, ribbon or raffia (straw-like material) through it. Send your bookmark master to schools before your visit so it can be duplicated and used as a handout. See sample in Chapter Three.

Book Order Form - This pre-order form is essential to increase sales when you visit schools. Author coordinators copy and distribute the form to students and staff before your event. The form includes your book's title, price, and a short description of your book and presentation. See sample in Chapter Three.

Book Reviews - Your publisher will probably send you favorable reviews about your book, but it's still a good idea to check in periodically for new ones. Use an X-ACTO® Knife and a ruler to cut and paste your best reviews onto white paper. Cut out the title of the publication and mount it at the top of the page. Then cut out the body of the review and position it below the title. Cut close to the text for best copying results. If black cut lines still appear after you've made a copy, use liquid paper correction fluid to cover them, and then duplicate the clean copy. See sample in Chapter Three.

Brochure - A good brochure is your most important and basic sales tool. It's a publicity piece for the press, bookstores, libraries, schools and conferences, and a promotional piece for display tables at educator, library, bookseller and other literary events.

In the beginning your brochure will include your headshot, biographical information, photo of your book, information about your book, a description of your school or conference presentation, review blurbs, contact telephone number, address, e-mail, and web site address.

Later, you may add media excerpts, descriptions of additional presentations, testimonials, awards, and honors. See sample in Chapter Three.

Business Cards - Your product is your book. Your service is what you do at bookstores, schools, libraries, and conferences. In order to promote your product and your services you'll need a business card just like any other professional. Desktop publishing and designer stationery make this easier than ever.

When it comes to designing your business card remember this law of the jungle: *Bad graphics are worse than no graphics.* But if you have some dynamic, eye-catching artwork that tells potential clients about you or your book, by all means include it. Author-illustrator Carol Heyer makes stickers of her original art and attaches them to her card for a dramatic effect. Some companies will put your color photo on your card at a reasonable price. It's gutsy—and memorable. It is no longer considered amateurish to put "writer" on your card, so go ahead and include it.

Calendar - You will need one central place to record your book signings, speaking engagements, appointments, telephone conversations, mileage, etc. I recommend a daily planner because it's portable. Keep only one calendar; otherwise you're bound to scribble something on one that you forgot to write on the other. Why double your work? If you prefer to keep personal engagements separately, just write them in different color ink. There are several models available. My personal favorite is the Franklin Daily Planner.

Content Sheet aka ***One-Sheet*** - A content sheet is an 8½" x 11" page used by professional speakers to describe each presentation. It typically contains a title in white letters on a black background spanning the top of the page, benefits to the audience, your headshot or book cover photo, a brief bio as it pertains to the presentation, testimonials, and contact information. See samples in Chapter Three.

Copyright Permission - If you don't own the rights to the artwork or photographs in your book, be sure to obtain permission from the artist or photographer before using them in any promotional materials. Otherwise, you can get yourself into big trouble.

Costume - Dressing up for public appearances is part of the fun. Costumes enhance your image and make you and your book memorable to your audiences. See samples in Chapter Eight.

Cover Letter - The cover letter concisely introduces you and what you have to offer to the media, conference program director, school principal, PTA, or anyone else to whom you send your promotional material. See samples in Chapter Three.

Desktop Publishing - You can save a lot of money by publishing your own promotional material. Ask colleagues and friends which programs they use and like.

Display Material - Display items may be made of acrylic, metal or wood. They will help you organize and feature your promotional pieces in a professional manner.

Here are some items to consider:

- Brochure holder
- Business card holder
- Tablecloth
- Bookstand
- Easel to hold a poster

Echinacea - I swear by this herb. It boosts your immune system. Believe me, when you come into contact with tens of thousands of kids and adults each year on the promotion trail, you're going to be exposed to a lot of unwelcome bugs. I use echinacea as a preventative before school visits and conferences, or immediately after I've been exposed to hackers and sneezers. One word of caution; echinacea and other immune-system boosters should not be taken by those who have any form of auto-immune disease.

Evaluation Form - This form will be particularly useful when you begin giving presentations. Honest, anonymous reactions and suggestions from your audience will help you improve the quality of your public appearances. See sample in Chapter Eight.

Extra Bulb - If you do a slide-illustrated presentation *always carry an extra bulb* for your projector. They burn out, they break, and power surges cause them to crack. Trust me. You don't want to get caught in front of an audience unable to deliver an anticipated slideshow.

Fee Schedule - A fee schedule is a price list of all the presentations you offer, such as student assemblies, staff development, parent workshops, and conference talks. See sample in Chapter Three.

Firm Handshake - A limp handshake leaves an impression of self-doubt. In contrast, a firm handshake tells people that you are confident, secure, and know what you're talking about. In a good handshake you firmly grasp someone's hand, pump twice, make direct eye contact, and smile!

Flyers - Book stores and libraries often create flyers to announce author appearances. In cases where they don't, you can easily create a nifty flyer on your computer. I recommend a versatile 8½" x 11" format. It can be used as a handout, folded and sent out as a mailer, and it can be mounted directly onto a poster.

A flyer should include:

- Your name
- Your photo
- Book title
- A photo of the book cover
- A short description of your book
- Review blurbs
- A one-line description of your presentation
- The name of the store or library
- Location
- Date
- Time
- Telephone

Handouts - Workshop and staff development participants, and conference attendees need and expect handouts. A handout can be as simple as a list of the main points you cover or as elaborate as a how-to guide addressing the topic of your workshop. See samples in Chapter Eight.

Headshot - Are you ready for your close-up? An 8" x 10" or 5" x 7" black-and-white glossy photo is the industry standard. I prefer an 8" x 10" because it looks more impressive on posters and bulletin boards. Consider having yours taken by a professional. Reprint labs work directly from the photograph so you won't need the negative. Have the lab print your name and the title of your book at the bottom. If you ask a friend to take your headshot make sure he takes a head and shoulders shot, with the camera pointed down rather than up, for a more flattering angle. The focus must be sharp, and there should be enough contrast between your hair color and the background for it to reproduce well. You'll want to purchase your headshots in quantity to send to the media, bookstores, schools, libraries and conference organizers. The media are more likely to run a story if you include a photo. When scheduling events, you can send a photo ahead to promote your appearance in newspapers, on bulletin boards and posters. See sample in Chapter Three.

Inventory - It's a good idea to inventory 30-50 copies of your book. I carry a supply in my car to every event. On several occasions bookstores, schools and conferences have sold out of my book due to customer demand. Sometimes the shipment doesn't arrive in time or someone just forgets to bring them.

Jackets (Book) - Prior to the publication of your book ask your publisher to run 30-50 extra book jackets. These will come in handy for creating inexpensive yet professional-looking press kits and posters.

Kodak® Slide Projector - This can be a plus if you plan to do presentations at schools and libraries. Kids today are so inundated with fast-paced computers, video games, and MTV that holding their attention is a challenge. Computers and VCRs have made slide projectors obsolete at most schools, so you'll want to invest in your own.

Labels - These come in all shapes and sizes for addresses, shipping, etc., and can be purchased at any office supply store. I use shipping labels on a 10" x 13" white envelope for mailing out press kits, and created a colorful "Meet the Author" label for the cover of my press kit to send to schools. See sample in Chapter Three.

Laser Pointer - If you do slide-illustrated presentations a laser pointer can be a plus. It's high tech and more professional than physically touching the screen or pointing with a stick. Laser pointers can be purchased at office supply stores for $50-$100.

Letter of Recommendation - Whenever you make a public appearance at a school, library, or conference tell the organizer that you are putting together promotional material and request a letter of recommendation on the organization's letterhead. These glowing endorsements will come in handy when booking future events. See samples in Chapter Three.

Luggage Cart - An inexpensive cart can be purchased at any large office supply store. This item is indispensable for carrying your projector and display material to events.

Mailing List - You will want to contact people with news about your book and upcoming events. Your mailing list can include friends, colleagues, personal media contacts, teachers, librarians, and organizations that are interested in your subject matter.

Media List - You'll need to compile an A-list, a B-list, and a C-list of newspaper, radio, magazine, newsletter, and television resources. Contact them with press releases and other announcements.

Overhead aka ***Transparency*** - An overhead is a transparent sheet that is projected onto a screen with an overhead projector. Overheads are essential for staff development or parent workshops. Visuals reinforce your important points and help guide your audience through your presentation. If you make copies of overheads they can pull double-duty as handouts. See sample in Chapter Eight.

Pitch - The pitch is shorthand for a sales pitch. It's a concise, well-organized and effective verbal presentation designed to convince the buyer that he wants what you have to offer. You'd pitch a bookseller for a signing, an editor for a story, a librarian for a school visit, etc. See sample in Chapter Six.

Postcard - If you own the copyright to the cover of your book you can scan it and create postcards on your computer. Use these as advertisements, invitations to your publication party or as thank-you notes. If you don't own the copyright you must get written permission from the artist.

Posters - Many bookstore chains will provide a poster for your event. However, it's a good idea to make up a couple of generic posters to publicize your appearances at independent bookstores, libraries, and conferences. Posters are simple to design. All you need are your photo, book cover and a flyer announcing the event. Spray the backs with photographic Spray Mount® then place them on a poster board. Spray Mount® and poster board can be purchased at most office supply and art-and-crafts stores. The beauty of Spray Mount® is that it lifts off, so for each new event all you have to do is replace the flyer. You can also make an inexpensive 11" x 16" poster of the cover of your book. I took a copy of my book to Kinko's and asked them to enlarge it, mount it on poster board and attach a cardboard stand on the back to prop it up. They did the job for under $20.

Post-it® Notes - These are a great help at book signings. Ask people to clearly print the correct spelling of the name of the person to whom the book will be inscribed. This prevents you from having to buy your own books because you misspelled someone's name.

Press Clipping - This is an article about you or a review of your book that appears in the print media. The name refers to the act of clipping it out of the publication. See sample in Chapter Three.

Press Kit - You can put together an impressive press kit for relatively little money. Use extra book jackets you've obtained from your publisher as press kit covers. Use Spray Mount® to attach them to the front of inexpensive two-pocket portfolios. If you can't obtain book jackets make color copies of your book cover on a quality printer on photographic paper. If you don't own or can't borrow a state-of-the-art printer, try Kinko's or Mail Boxes, Etc. An alternative is to generate labels on your computer with your name and the title of your book.

A press kit includes:

- A cover letter
- A press release
- Copies of book reviews
- Your black-and-white glossy headshot
- A bio that reads like an interesting story
- A business card
- Your brochure
- A copy of your book (optional)

Voilá—you have a press kit! Before you write up a press release check with your publisher—someone may have already composed one. When possible, include a signed copy of your book for the media on your A-list. I make color copies of the full-page color ad in my publisher's catalog and include them in my press kit as well. See samples in Chapter Three.

Press Release aka ***News Release*** aka ***Media Release*** - A press release is written in a journalistic style. It is typed on one page and double-spaced. Media people are busy and need the facts up front. If you are flowery and verbose they may not read it to the end. The lead paragraph must tell who, what, where, when, and why. The second paragraph expands on the lead. Proceed with information in decreasing order of importance. Be sure to include your name, the name of your book, publisher, intended audience, price, ISBN number, and contact telephone number. Technically, a "press release" refers to a notice sent to the print media. A notice sent to television or radio is referred to as a "news release" or a "media release." See samples in Chapter Three.

Purell® Instant Hand Sanitizer - I shake a lot of hands at conferences, bookstore signings, library presentations, fund-raisers, and especially during school visits. I don't mean to sound like a germ-paranoid person but contact with all those hands adds up to a lot of bacteria. This stuff kills germs when you don't have access to soap, water, and towels.

Questionnaire (Author) - Prior to the publication of your book your publisher will send you an Author Questionnaire requesting background information, contacts and any other information that will help sell copies. Fill it out thoroughly and mail it in as soon as possible. If you fail to receive an Author Questionnaire, ask your publisher for one at least three months before the publication date.

Remote Control - If you decide to do a slide-illustrated presentation you'll need a wireless remote. Using a remote control that attaches to the projector with a wire is awkward and it limits your movements.

Schedule of Events - Start sending your publisher a monthly updated schedule as soon as you begin booking events. It not only helps them keep enough books on the shelves in geographical areas where you'll be presenting, it also shows them how enterprising you are. See sample in Chapter Two.

School Presentation Kit aka ***Press Kit*** - This is a presentation kit of materials provided to principals, librarians, PTA and school board members, cultural councils, and anyone else who expresses interest in booking you for an appearance. Your press kit easily converts into a school presentation kit. Simply replace the book jacket on the front of the portfolio with a computer-generated label that says, "Meet the Author" or "School Presentations by," then include your name and the title of your book. Since I purchase my headshots in quantity, I prefer to include one so that it can be used to promote my visit when they hire me. I call this package a "press kit" regardless of whom I send it to because it's a familiar term.

A school presentation kit includes:

- A cover letter
- One or more content sheets
- Copy of the publisher's catalog ad for your book
- Book reviews
- Brochure
- Letter of recommendation (if you have one)
- Business card

Spray Mount® - Frame shops use this adhesive spray to mount photographs. It's tacky—like Post-it® Notes—and allows you to lift and reposition photos, book covers, press clippings, flyers, and anything else that you cut and paste.

Stationery - Your letterhead and stationery are as much a part of your image as your business card and brochure. There should be uniformity to the appearance of all your promotional pieces. In addition to your name, address, and phone number, be sure to include your e-mail and web site addresses if you have them. Stay away from dark paper stock. It makes the type difficult to read and doesn't fax well.

Teacher's Guide - Creating a Teacher's Guide with suggestions on how to incorporate your book into the curriculum will encourage educators to use your book in the classroom. Come up with ideas for as many subject areas as possible.

Thank-You Notes - Organizing an event involves preparation, effort and coordination. Take time to thank your host in writing.

Two-Pocket Portfolio - This is a fancy name for the color folder in which you put your press material. They come in matte and glossy paper. Stationery and office supply stores carry them. I buy mine in quantity for pennies apiece when they go on sale. Glossy folders are considerably more expensive.

Voice Mail - Check your messages every day. A professional always returns phone calls in a timely fashion. If you don't, word gets around fast that you're unreliable.

Web Site - Many authors have web sites. Establish a presence now—before the deluge. Add your web site address to all your promotional material. Visit my web site at www.evegallardo.com.

Window Display - A window display will help attract customers to a bookstore signing. I provide booksellers with orangutan, gorilla, chimpanzee and monkey stuffed animals, hanging vines, a length of cloth with a jungle pattern, and a poster. Your display will depend upon the subject of your book. Be creative.

X-ACTO® Knife - This is an artists' tool that will help you precisely cut and paste book reviews, press clippings, and other promotional material for professional, clean-looking copies.

You - Let's not overlook the obvious. *You* are your book's best tool, promoter, and best friend. No one else can promote your book with as much energy and passion as you.

Zeal - Enthusiasm is contagious!

Phase 2

Expedition Briefing

Chapter Two

Author in the Mist
Working with Your Publisher

Publishers all have horror stories about working with problem authors who make unrealistic demands. Don't approach your publisher beating your chest like King Kong and demand a book tour, a guest appearance on Larry King Live, and a full-page ad in the New York Times. You won't get much support that way. Instead, use gentle persuasion. An *"I want to help you sell my book and this is what I'm willing to do"* approach will go a lot further than using a *"Now what are you going to do for me?"* attitude.

The realities of the publishing world are that buy-outs, mergers, and takeovers create huge conglomerates that force first-time authors into the literary mist. Most publicity departments are overworked and understaffed. At smaller publishing houses, the marketing department often *is* the publicity department. With more than 1.5 million titles in print and 60,000 new books slated for publication in 2000, the sheer number of authors coupled with limited promotion dollars makes it impossible for publishers to promote each book equally—if at all. Depending on the publisher, your ideas will be greeted with varying degrees of enthusiasm. Smaller publishers are generally more receptive. But regardless of their reaction, don't take it personally and don't be discouraged. You can still help promote your book in several important ways.

Contacting Your Publisher

Save telephone calls for timely matters or exceptionally good news. Otherwise, communicate via e-mail, fax or snail-mail. I often find answers to my questions by checking my publisher's web site at

12

www.chroniclebooks.com. Chronicle Books lists its trade show calendar, Top Ten books, and more. When I noticed that a staff member had chosen my book for the Top Ten list, I thanked her via e-mail. When Teacher Guides became a new feature, I mailed in the one I'd written. When you start booking events, e-mail your schedule at the top of every month. Chronicle, like many publishers, includes an Author Touring Schedule on their web site. The only way your publisher can post your events is if you keep them informed. Here is an excerpt from a schedule of events I sent to my publisher.

Evelyn Gallardo's Schedule of Events
Winter 2000-Spring 2000 (as of January 13, 2000)

Thursday January 13	Hurley Elementary 536 S. Laura Ave. La Puente, CA 91744	Becky Neufeld	626-555-5555
Wednesday January 19	O.C. Johnson Elem. 1201 W. 12th St. Yuma, AZ 85364	Virginia Rascon	520-555-5555
Thursday January 20	Lightfoot Elementary 6989 Kenyon Way Alta Loma, CA 91701	Rosann Marlen	909-555-5555
Saturday January 22	Manhattan Beach Lib. 1320 Highland Ave. M. B., CA 90266	Cindy Roth	310-555-5555

Author Questionnaire

Long before your book hits the stores your publisher will send you an Author Questionnaire. It's critical that you fill it out completely and return it as soon as possible because it will be used as a resource for press releases, flap copy and in contacting your local media.

You will be asked to provide a list of your local newspapers, radio and television stations, local and regional magazines, community leaders, and influential friends. In other words, contacts not already in your publisher's files. To get the names of media contacts, just call their main offices and ask who handles stories about local authors.

You'll also need to compile a list of contacts in your book's subject category. If, for example, it's a nonfiction book about animals, list nonprofit organizations, zoos, natural history museums, and other special interest groups. Be expansive and creative. Include any group or individual who might be interested in reading your book. Your publisher may not send review copies to all of them, but it's worth a try. Like chicken soup, too much can't hurt, and it might help. Here are a few of the contacts I listed.

The Daily Breeze	Orangutan Foundation Int'l.	Los Angeles Zoo
5212 Torrance Blvd.	822 S. Wellesley Ave.	5333 Zoo Drive
Torrance, CA 90509	Los Angeles, CA 90049	Los Angeles, CA 90027
310-540-5511	800-ORANGUTAN	323-666-4650

Now, list three of your local media contacts:

1. _____
2. _____
3. _____

List three nonprofit organizations related to your book:

1. _____
2. _____
3. _____

List three special interest groups related to your book:

1. _____
2. _____
3. _____

Add as many other contacts as you can, transfer them to your Author Questionnaire, then mail them to your publisher.

Making Friends

Call your publisher's marketing department and get acquainted with whoever is in charge of publicity and author events. Let them know what you are willing to do. Will you visit schools, speak at conferences, sign books at trade shows, do interviews or participate in other events? Again, response varies, but many publishers, especially smaller ones, are thrilled with an author who volunteers to promote her book and trek the trail less traveled.

Here's what I said when I called my publisher's Children's Marketing and Sales Department:

"Hi, this is Evelyn Gallardo, the author of *Among the Orangutans*. I know you're busy but do you have a minute to talk? Great! I used to be a Sales Promotions Manager for an international firm. I know what it takes to sell a product and I'm willing to do it. I want to help you sell my book. I love doing school visits and will be booking several of my own. Please put me on your list of available authors when you get calls from schools. I'm also happy to do bookstore signings, conference speaking engagements, signings at local trade shows, and media interviews. My goal is to push my book into a second printing. Feel free to contact me about any events I can participate in. Thanks, I really appreciate your time."

Now, write a draft of what you plan to say when you call your publisher:

_____

_____

_____

_____

_____

_____

_____

Reps

Contacting your local sales rep falls into a delicate area. Reps are on the road much of the time and are hard pressed when it comes to returning phone calls from authors. Many a rep has been burned by a new author whose approach was as welcome as a squirt of mosquito repellent in the eye. Don't take it personally if your calls are not returned. I interviewed several reps and asked them how authors and reps could work together. Without exception, each one got a glazed look in his or her eye and began stammering. The response was underwhelming. What they all seem to need is more hours in the day to complete the work at hand. So, I recommend a hands-off approach. E-mail or fax your rep a copy of your schedule of events with a personal note, "Just keeping you informed. Feel free to let your stores know I'm available for book signings and school visits." Or send a Christmas card saying, "Thanks for all your efforts." Some of my colleagues got creative and invited their mutual rep out to lunch and he accepted. There's always the exception. Another way to make friends with reps without intruding on their precious time is at events. Just remember to keep your conversation brief, to the point, and graciously step aside when a potential customer approaches.

Events

Publishers generally staff their booths with marketing and sales people, and this is a good time to introduce yourself. But keep in mind that they are there to sell all the books on their list, not just yours. Save the friendly chitchat for down times.

Don't expect your publisher to fly you to out-of-town events. But if Book Expo America (BEA) or the American Library Association (ALA) is coming to your town—and your publisher is participating—call ahead and offer to sign your book at their booth. While at the booth, don't just sit there! Make it easy for people to approach you. Initiate eye contact and don't hesitate to speak first. I always smile, lean forward, extend a hand and say, *"Hi, I'm your local children's author. I don't get out of my office very often. Come on over and meet me."* No one has ever left me with my hand dangling like a vine in midair.

If no author is scheduled after you, offer to stay past your designated time. Always be willing to do more than you promised. I worked my publisher's booth at ALA so hard one year that when I mentioned that having a bookmark would save me from signing hundreds of bits of paper at schools, they produced 10,000 beautiful ones for me.

Things You Can and Should Ask For

Prior to the printing of your book you can request that your publisher run 30-50 extra covers for posters and press kits. Ask for black-and-white photos of your book cover as well. These can be used for promotion in nonprofit organization catalogs, newsletters, or school newspapers. You can also request complimentary and review copies of your book to send to personal contacts. If your publisher makes brochures for authors, ask for copies in quantity. If they don't provide brochures, make up your own and ask how many *they'd* like to have. It's a good idea to get copies of your book at every stage in case you ever decide to do a presentation on the publication process. This can include, but is not limited to, galleys, F & G's (fold & gathers), a signature (16 pages on one sheet before it's cut), and a copy of a preliminary sketch by the illustrator. Let your publisher know your intentions well in advance and ask that this material be mailed to you. Ask questions about what else is available that might help you demonstrate the process.

Book Award Submissions

Winning an award is a great excuse to send out a press release and gain attention for your book. Do your research. *Writer's Market, Literary Market Place,* and *Children's Books Awards & Prizes* published by the Children's Book Council are all excellent resources. Provide your publisher with a list of awards for which your book is eligible. With enough lead-time you can call or write ahead to the awards committee for submission guidelines. In most cases, your publisher must submit your book.

This is a partial listing of what I sent to my publisher. I used an easy-to-fax-back format to help my publisher keep me apprised of submissions.

To: Nan Davis

Fr: Evelyn Gallardo

Re: Book Awards

May I help make your job easier? After careful research, I've come up with the following awards for which my book is eligible. A star next to a listing indicates I sent away for, and received the included information. Please submit *Among the Orangutans* for the following awards. I've provided a space in front of each listing so you can fax back to me as submissions are made. Thank you so much for all your hard work to help make our book a success!

Date Submitted	Award
_____	California Children's Book, Video, and Software Award
_____	Christopher Awards*
_____	Golden Kite Awards*
_____	Judy Lopez Memorial Award*
_____	Orbis Pictus Award for Outstanding Nonfiction for Children*
_____	Young Readers Choice Awards

Using the resources I described, list six awards and prizes for which your book is eligible.

1. _____

2. _____

3. _____

4. _____

5. _____

6. _____

Now, add at least six more to your list and e-mail or fax them to your publisher.

Additional Printings

I let my publisher know early on that my goal was to get my book into a second printing. I assured them that I would aggressively seek bookings for school visits, speak at conferences, and generate interviews with the media.

Periodically you should check with your publisher's marketing and sales department to find out how many of your books are left. When stock goes below a thousand I start to get nervous. I always let my publisher know about upcoming events and situations that might affect sales. For instance, 6 months before the subject of my biography, Dr. Biruté Galdikas, celebrated her twenty-fifth anniversary of researching orangutans, I called my publishing company and made it aware of this event and the publicity it would generate, a sure booster for book sales. They responded by ordering another printing of my book. The point is—don't expect your publisher to automatically go into a second printing—even if the first one sells out. Take the lead and plant the seed yourself.

In Conclusion

It will take time to nurture relationships with people in the marketing, sales, and publicity departments. Ask for specific names of who to contact for specific needs. Always be courteous and enthusiastic. Keep conversations and correspondence short and to the point. Don't beat your chest like King Kong or shriek like Fay Wray if you don't get your way. Smile and try another approach. And always remember the laws of the jungle: *Keep your publisher apprised of your plans, follow up verbal requests in writing, and send copies of any materials that you produce. Nobody likes surprises.*

Chapter Three

Beat Your Tom-Tom
Create Promotion Material with Pizzazz

Primates, like the rest of our kin in the animal kingdom, use several methods to attract the opposite sex. After all, propagation prevents extinction.

Mature male orangutans develop large throat pouches used as resonators to help them make the "long-call," a mating vocalization that attracts females. The long-call can be heard from two miles away. They also develop saucer-like cheekpads on their face. Females are drawn to the males with the largest cheekpads. If you're a male orangutan and you don't have them, females won't even glance your way. A female will ignore an immature male in favor of a cheek-padder every time. When she hears the long-call, she'll cross rivers, swamps, and miles of impenetrable forest to tweak his large and impressive cheekpads—an unmistakable sign she's interested in propagating the species.

Male gorillas strut bipedally, beat their chest, and roar until they shake the jungle floor. They also develop a striking silver saddle of fur across their back as a physical signal of maturity. I once watched a lone male silverback named Tiger strut and roar, then snap a fat branch from a tree and slap it repeatedly against the ground with all the bluster he could muster. This bachelor had been following a group of gorillas for several days, trying to entice females away from his competitor with displays of prowess. Beethoven, the aging leader of Group 5, had responded with chest beats and roars of his own. Poppy, a young female in the group, had watched the display with intense interest. In the end, she crossed a ravine and joined Tiger on the neighboring hill. Tiger's persistence and impressive display had won him a wife.

Whether it's chest beating, long-calls or roars—these apes are all doing the same thing—pounding their tom-toms to advertise their availability. Their cheekpads, silver fur and displays are designed to attract. If you want to prevent your book from becoming extinct after just one printing, you'll need to design promotion material to court the media, schools, libraries and conferences coordinators. Each carefully crafted piece is a drumbeat that tells people that you and your book are terrific. Your promotion material reflects the quality of what you have to offer. A half-hearted attempt with poorly executed material is like a male orangutan trying to attract a female before he has developed his cheekpads and throat pouch.

In this chapter I will explain how to create quality promotion material, show you examples, and provide the building blocks to help you craft your own. You owe it to yourself, your clients, and your audience to strut your best stuff. So go ahead, beat your promotional drum loudly, but make sure it's the best-looking tom-tom in the jungle.

Press Kit

Your press kit is where you display your prowess—all that you and your book are, promise to be, and are capable of delivering. You don't have to spend a fortune on professional printing. You can put together an impressive press kit for under $1.00. If you want to really get fancy, you might spend up to $3.00. Scanners, printers and desktop publishing have improved tremendously since the writing of this book's first edition. Use your home technology to the fullest. The key here is to remember you're putting together a package. It should have a cohesive look and feel. You may want to choose a photo, logo or graphic to use as a recurring theme throughout your press kit. I use a photo of an orangutan hanging on my back to attract the reader's attention. Each component is part of a whole and serves a specific purpose. When you begin booking speaking engagements, your press kit will pull double duty when you add content sheets, a fee schedule, etc. First we'll concentrate on a press kit geared toward the media, and then we'll discuss the add-ins geared toward cultivating speaking engagements at schools, libraries and conferences.

Because you will package your material in a two-pocket portfolio, we'll begin by covering the components of the right-hand pocket, then the left. The right-hand pocket contains information primarily about you and includes your cover letter, bio, etc. The left-hand pocket concentrates more on your book and is comprised of a press release, book reviews, etc. Let's navigate through each piece and see what's involved.

Two-Pocket Portfolio

This is the fancy name for the folders in which you place your press material. They come both in matte and glossy finishes. Stationery stores sell them individually at a higher price, and office supply chain stores often market them in bundles of 10 at a bargain price. I've bought the less expensive matte folders in quantity for as little 13 cents apiece. The glossy folders are considerably more expensive and can cost between $1.00 and $2.99 each. The choice is yours. You have two options on how to design the portfolio cover so people will know at a glance what's inside.

Book Jacket

Prior to the physical publication of your book, ask your publisher to run 30-50 extra book jackets. These will come in handy for creating economical, yet professional-looking press kit covers. Trim the jackets with an X-acto® Knife, lightly spray the back with adhesive Spray Mount®, then position the cover on the front of the two-pocket portfolio. Don't worry if it isn't quite centered the first time. Spray Mount® lifts off, allowing you to reposition the jacket. If you can't get extra book jackets from your publisher, make color copies of your book cover on a quality printer on quality photographic paper. You may have to test different brands of paper to get the best reproduction. An alternative is to generate labels on your computer.

Labels

Labels come in all sizes such as, address, shipping, etc., and can be purchased in quantity at any office supply store. They can be simple and one color, printed with your name and the title of your book. I wanted to save my book jackets for the media, so I used Avery® 3⅓″ x 4″ shipping labels to create a colorful "Meet the Author" label for the press kit I sent to schools. Labels can be easily produced from most software programs.

Meet the Author

Follow Your Dream

★ Student Assembly   ★ Staff Development   ★ Parent Workshop
with the author of...
Among the Orangutans
Evelyn Gallardo

Now, design your own label:

Right-hand Pocket

Brochure

When a press kit is first opened, the human eye is automatically drawn to the right-hand pocket. The first item a potential client should see is your brochure. You must think of everyone who receives your promotion material as a potential client, whether you're trying to sell that person on writing a story, arranging a book signing, or hiring you as a speaker. A good brochure is your most important and basic sales tool. Like a Swiss army knife with all its gadgets, a well-written brochure serves several purposes. It's a publicity piece for the press, bookstores and libraries, a hire-me-they'll-love-me advertisement for schools and conferences, and a promotional piece for display tables at educator, library, bookseller and other literary events. I waited six months after my book was published to produce my first brochure. Don't make the same mistake. Start working on yours now, even if your book is months away from publication. When it does hit the stands—you'll be prepared.

When designing your brochure, use headings in larger type and leave some white space between sections to make it more inviting to the eye. Tightly compacted paragraphs appear too time-consuming to read and you'd be surprised how many people won't bother. Once, after running 5,000 copies of my updated brochure, I realized I'd forgotten to include my web site and e-mail addresses. Luckily, I'd left enough white space around my contact information to run the brochures through my computer's printer with the added critical elements. I recommend an 8½ " x 11" trifold format. It's professional, fits in a standard envelope, and gives you six panels to work with. Forget odd sizes and fancy folds. They cost more to mail and produce, and serve no real purpose. You can create your brochure on any number of desktop publishing formats. I use Microsoft Word. If you don't own a scanner, you can have your photos scanned at a full-service copy shop, then transfer them to the brochure. Copy your brochure onto a disk then take it to a reputable printer for duplication and folding.

Since I distribute my brochures like pollen, I use a post office box rather than my home address. The choice is yours. If your publisher books its authors for events, you may also want to list contact information for its publicity department, but be sure to get permission first.

In the beginning, your brochure will include:

- Your headshot
- Biographical information
- Photo of your book
- Information about your book
- A description of your school or conference presentation
- Review blurbs
- Contact telephone number, address, e-mail, web site address

Later you may add:

- Media excerpts
- Descriptions of additional presentations
- Testimonials
- Awards
- Honors

It's a good idea to visit bookstores and attend conferences and collect other authors' brochures. Study them and see how your colleagues get their point across. Which style and layout do you prefer? Stand back at conferences and pay attention to the brochures people pick up most frequently. I noticed at one event that out of several brochures on display, people consistently reached for the one that said, "Meet the Author," in bold print. Many desktop publishing programs have templates for brochures, so it's much easier to create your own than you might think. I had to be dragged into the computer age kicking and screaming. I was terrified of learning a program and doing my first brochure. But I'll tell you, after creating that first one, I became a brochure-producing fool and have created many since then. If I can do it, so can you.

After you review my brochure on the following page, come back and compose a rough draft for your own in the spaces provided below. Although reproduced in black and white for the purposes of this book, my actual brochure has three photos in color. You can add color inexpensively by leaving a blank space where you would like to insert a color photo. Take your disk or master, minus the color photos, to a professional printer and have him run copies without folding them. A simple way to add color in the right spots is to call up the file on your computer where you produced the brochure and insert the scanned photos in the blank spots. Then delete any text or photos that are in black ink, leaving only the color photos. Caution: Click "Save as," and save the file with only the color photos under a name like "Brochure Photos." (This is a critical step. You *must* save the photos under a different name. You want to end up with two files, not delete your original brochure file!) You can then physically run your brochure through your computer's color printer, click "print," and print your color photos directly onto them. You'll only spend a couple of hundred dollars having a professional print your brochure in black ink, whereas you would pay him several thousand dollars to do it in color.

Now, take the first steps to create your own brochure. Write a pithy attention-grabber for the front panel.

_____

_____

_____

_____

_____

_____

List any photos you can use or need to take for your brochure. _____

_____

_____

Compose your "About the Author" information. _____

_____

_____

_____

_____

_____

_____

_____

_____

_____

_____

Write a short description of your book. _____

_____

_____

_____

_____

Include excerpts from your best reviews. _____

_____

_____

_____

_____

Describe your book-related presentation(s) for schools, libraries and/or conferences. _____

_____

_____

_____

_____

Include testimonials for your presentation(s) if you have them. _____

_____

_____

_____

_____

List your credits including books and/or articles. _____

_____

_____

_____

Write your "how to contact me" information. Don't forget your e-mail and web site addresses.

_____

_____

_____

Meet the Author

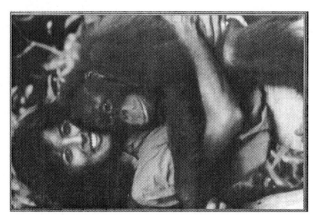

How to Promote Your Children's Book

Books

Among the Orangutans
Chronicle Books, 1993
How to Promote Your Children's Book
Primate Productions, 1997
Endangered Wildlife
Contributing Author
GINN Publishing Canada, 1993
Jane Goodall's Animal World: Gorillas
Contributing Photographer, Atheneum, 1990

Photos

The Dark Romance of Dian Fossey,
McGraw Hill, Science Magazine, Animal
Magazine, GEO, L.A. Times, Terre Sauvage,
American Greeting Cards, PongoQuest, Zoolife.
National Wildlife Federation, Ranger Rick

Documentary

Orangutans: Grasping the Last Branch
Co-Producer, Primate Productions, 1993

---

*"This is a good resource for writers.
I gave one to a friend."*
—Paula Danziger, *Amber Brown is Not a Crayon*

*"Evelyn is the queen of book promotion. She's
proof that an author or illustrator's promotional
efforts really can make a difference."*
—Bruce Balan, *Buoy, Home at Sea*

*"When I followed Evelyn's advice, the effort
I put into promoting my book really paid off."*
—Gennifer Choldenko, *Moonstruck*

To arrange school and conference
appearances, writer's consultations,
and media interviews, contact:

Primate Productions
P.O. Box 3038
Manhattan Beach, CA 90266

(310) 545-9582

Evelyn Gallardo

Follow Your Dream

is Evelyn's theme. She has visited 350
schools and inspired more than 300,000
students throughout the world.

This bilingual author-photographer
combines a love of travel with a passion
for critically endangered primates.
She has worked in Rwanda with gorilla
researcher Dr. Dian Fossey and in
Borneo with orangutan authority
Dr. Biruté Galdikas.

Armed with Evelyn's no-nonsense arsenal
of tactics, both new and seasoned writers learn
how to sell more books, increase their incomes
and have a grand time doing it!

Evelyn conducts book promotion workshops,
seminars and individual consultations. See full
panel for contact information. Her children's book,
Among the Orangutans, is in its fourth printing.

Among the Orangutans

Among the Orangutans is a biography of Biruté Galdikas, a scientist who devotes her life to studying and preserving the endangered wild orangutan and its rain forest habitat. A student of Dr. Louis Leakey, and a colleague of both Jane Goodall and Dian Fossey, Biruté Galdikas is the world's authority on the life and behavior of the mysterious orangutan.

"It will rouse reader of all ages!"
—Publisher's Weekly

"Excellent! Children will love it."
—National Geographic

"It grabs readers right from the cover."
—Booklure

Awards and Honors

◆ Color Me Bright "North Star Award"
◆ Nueva Award
◆ John Burroughs Outstanding Nature Book
◆ Dian Fossey Gorilla Fund
◆ LAUSD Superintendent's Commendation
   Awarded by Ruben Zacarias

Presentations

Let student imaginations soar in the author's award-winning "Follow Your Dream" Assembly. Evelyn has been charged by a gorilla on a Rwandan volcano, has helped return an orphan orangutan to the Borneo rain forest, and has slept at the zoo in Uganda. Storytelling, captivating photos, ape vocalizations, world cultures, and careers in writing, science and photography all contribute to this unforgettable experience.

"We still hear her gorilla vocalizations repeated in the hallways!"
—Barbara Bersteinsson, Cornerstone School

"Her visit worked on so many important levels: writing, science, conservation, geography, role model. I could go on and on!"
—Brad Rumble, Rosemont Elementary

"Follow Your Dream is a quality presentation. Ms. Gallardo meets the needs of her audience."
—Joanne Hickey, Lincoln Int'l School of Uganda

Support Workshops

◆ **Create a Photo-Illustrated Book**—Students
◆ **Writing Workshop**—Staff Development
◆ **Help Your Child Create a Photo-Illustrated Book**—Parents

Conferences

◆ California Reading Association
◆ California School Library Association
◆ UC Irvine Writer's Conference
◆ Claremont Young Writer's Conference
◆ LAUSD Title VII Conference
◆ California School Board Association
◆ L.A. Times Book Festival

About the Author

Evelyn Gallardo's fascination with primates stems from childhood, "My first crush was King Kong." But it was movies such as "Tarzan" and her middle school teacher's trek through South America that fueled Evelyn's love for travel. She has visited Rwanda, Uganda, Borneo, Kenya, Nepal, India, Mexico, China, Japan, Java, Costa Rica and South America where she explored the Galapagos Islands, Macchu Picchu, Iguazu Falls, and hitched cargo boats up the Amazon.

Another driving force in this Los Angeles-born author's life is her Mexican-Hopi heritage. "My great-grandparents infused me with a love for our culture." She teaches a Mexican American Culture Inservice to help educators better understand their students. Her current writing projects include picture books, poetry and nonfiction. Evelyn studied with National Geographic photographers and is a graduate of UCLA Extension's Creative Writing Program.

She is on the board of Friends of Children and Literature (FOCAL) and is the West Coast Representative of the International Primate Protection League. She is a founding member of the Children's Authors Network and a member of the Author's Guild, PEN, Society of Children's Book Writers & Illustrators, and the Orangutan Foundation International.

Now, for those of you who have never created a brochure on your computer before, come out of hibernation, take that first scary step out of the cave and start learning how to do it in your favorite program. There are worse things. You aren't jumping into the Amazon and fighting a 30-foot anaconda, after all. Congratulations. You're on your way!

Cover Letter

Your cover letter goes behind your brochure. It introduces you in concise terms and tells recipients why you are sending your press kit and why they should take time out from their busy schedule to read it.

Dear Reporter,

I enjoyed meeting you on the telephone today and discussing my new book, *Among the Orangutans*, a biography of Biruté Galdikas. As you'll recall Dr. Galdikas is a scientist who has devoted her life to studying protecting, and preserving the endangered wild orangutan and its rain forest habitat.

As I mentioned, I'm a local resident and have lived in Manhattan Beach for 16 years. You will find a press kit and copy of my book enclosed, as promised. What may be of particular interest to your readers is that I traveled to Borneo, worked as a volunteer on the Orangutan Project, and took many of the photographs myself. Do I have stories to tell!

Thank you for taking the time to review the enclosed material. I have enjoyed the many environmental articles covered in the Beach Reporter over the years. If my new book is something you believe your readers will find of interest, I am available for an interview. I look forward to hearing from you soon.
Regards,

Evelyn Gallardo

Headshot

Your headshot comes next. The headshot is an important component for the media. They are more likely to run a story that has an accompanying photo. Perhaps there is no photographer available the day you are interviewed. Maybe the reporter took his own photos and they weren't acceptable for one reason or another. An 8" x 10" or 5" x 7" black-and-white glossy photo is standard. I prefer an 8" x 10" because it's more impressive on posters and bulletin boards when you send it to schools and libraries. Consider having your headshot taken by a professional. I've seen many shots taken by spouses or friends and frankly, they look amateurish. If you aren't convinced, look through any conference catalog. Can you spot the photos taken by Uncle Burt or Aunt Sadie in the backyard? The choice is yours, but remember that any flaw in the photo will be magnified when it's enlarged.

Reprint labs work directly from the photograph so you won't need the negative. Have the lab print your name and the title of your book(s) at the bottom. You'll want to purchase your headshots in quantity to send to the media, bookstores, schools, libraries and conference organizers. The higher the quantity you purchase, the lower the cost per unit. I recommend ordering around 300. Your appearance may change or you may have a new book out before you go through 1,000 headshots.

Evelyn Gallardo

Author of *Among the Orangutans—The Biruté Galdikas Story*, Chronicle Books

Bio

You bio should read like an interesting literary piece. It can range from 1-3 pages. I prefer a 1-page bio because busy people like their information in digestible chunks. Also, when you call program directors about speaking at conferences and other events, they may ask you to fax it. Often faxes are hard to read, so make the recipient's job as easy as possible. A well-written bio is like a good compass—it leads the reader directly to a predetermined destination, whether it's writing a story about you or hiring you as a speaker. Your lead paragraph will feature your prominent accomplishments as they relate to your book. Are you a spelunker who has written a book on cave exploration? The body of the bio includes recent achievements, highlights in your childhood, place of birth, education and other interesting bits of information pertaining to your book. Conclude with an upbeat paragraph that looks to the future. Here's my bio.

Evelyn Gallardo
2208 The Strand, B
Manhattan Beach, CA 90266
(310) 545-9582   Fax: (310) 545-8218
Web site: www.evegallardo.com   e-mail: EveGal22@aol.com

Bio

There are writers, wildlife photographers, adventurers, conservationists, and linguists. But rarely are they all found in one person. That person is Evelyn Gallardo. Her specialty, close-up photographs of endangered apes, has brought her eye-to-eye with gorillas, chimpanzees, and orangutans in places as remote as Rwanda, Uganda, and Borneo. Evelyn's photographs have appeared in *Jane Goodall's Animal World: Gorillas, The Dark Romance of Dian Fossey,* Science Magazine, Animal Magazine, GEO, PongoQuest, Endangered Wildlife, Terre Sauvage, and in college textbooks, calendars, and greeting cards around the world. She is represented by Peter Arnold Photo Agency in New York.

Her passion for great apes and other primates was kindled during childhood by movies such as "King Kong" and "Mighty Joe Young." And while other girls her age were reading Nancy Drew, Evelyn was devouring the *Tarzan* book series, fanning an ember to travel around the world. During the mid-seventies she spent nine months trekking through South America, where she hitched cargo boats up the Amazon with her husband, David, and her five-year-old daughter, Dawn. Uganda, Rwanda, Kenya, Zaire, Borneo, Bali, Sumba, Nepal, India, China, Costa Rica, and Mexico are among the many other exotic places she has visited. In 1984, a trip to Borneo as a volunteer on the Orangutan Project inspired her to write *Among the Orangutans,* which is now in a fourth printing. In addition to receiving a starred review in Publisher's Weekly, her book was honored with the "John Burroughs Outstanding Nature Book Award" and the "Nueva Award." She is also the author of *How to Promote Your Children's Book—A Survival Guide for Published Writers*. Evelyn's numerous articles have appeared in newspapers, magazines, and conservation newsletters around the world.

Another driving force in this bilingual Mexican-Hopi writer's life is her desire to inspire inner-city children to follow their wildest dreams and to explore how they can make positive contributions to the planet. In the past fourteen years she has visited more than 400 schools worldwide and inspired more than 300,000 students. For her exceptional work with children and in conservation, Evelyn was presented the Color Me Bright Youth Foundation's "North Star Award," the Orangutan Foundation's "International Service Award," and the Dian Fossey Gorilla Foundation's "Outstanding Support for Anti-Poaching Award."

Evelyn's current writing projects include *Journey of a Wildlife Photographer*, *African Wildlife Vet*, and a children's picture book based on her heritage. She will soon appear in an educational video series, "The Write Stuff," for use in fourth and fifth grade classrooms. Evelyn studied nature photography at UCLA and graduated from the UCLA Extension Creative Writing Program.

Now, write your own bio.

Name _____

Address _____

Phone_____Fax_____E-mail_____Website _____

Begin with a "grabber" that describes you and your prominent accomplishments as they pertain to your book.

_____

_____

Describe your recent achievements. _____

_____

_____

_____

Give a brief synopsis of your book. _____

_____

_____

Describe your childhood featuring highlights that pertain to your book. _____

_____

_____

_____

End with an upbeat paragraph about the future. _____

_____

_____

_____

_____

Newspaper Articles

Insert any articles that have been written about you and/or your book behind your bio. If you have yet to make your press debut, a good alternative is to include a clean copy of a recent article particularly pertinent to your book's topic. Another alternative is to cut and paste titles of several relevant articles onto an 8½" x 11" sheet and copy it. This demonstrates your book is newsworthy.

Left-hand Pocket

Business Card

Most two-pocket portfolios contain slits where you can insert your business card. Always design your business card in the standard 2" x 3½" size. Cutting your card into an odd size can be annoying for the recipient. It won't fit into wallet sleeves or other business card holders. There are plenty of programs and designer stationery choices to help you with your design. Another law of the jungle is this: *No graphics are better than bad graphics.* If you find a playful, elegant, or childlike font you like, you can use it as a graphic. In that case, print your name larger in the font, but guard against overkill. You may want to use a standard and easy-to-read font such as Times New Roman for the rest of the card. You can have too much of a good thing if people have to struggle to read the fine print.

Press Release

A press release can announce the publication of a new book, an award, a speaking engagement, or some other newsworthy event. It is written in a journalistic style. Technically, a "press release" refers to a notice sent to the print media. A notice sent to television or radio is referred to as "news release" or a "media release." It is typed on one page and double-spaced. The double-spaced format is easier to read and allows an editor to add notes between the lines. Media people are busy and need the facts up front. The lead paragraph must tell who, what, where, when, and why. The second paragraph expands on the lead. Proceed with

Daily Breeze

Torrance, California
102nd year/Number 345
© 1996 The Copley Press Inc.

TUESDAY

Zest For Life

AUTHOR-ACTIVIST
EMPOWERS CHILDREN
TO DO THEIR BEST

LIFE/ARTS D1

Gallardo has spent the last 10 years talking to students, such as these at Braddock Drive Elementary School, about her work among the apes, about writing and about her Mexican-Hopi cultural background.

Message of
EMPOWERMENT

Wildlife activist instills zest for caring, success to children

By Verne Palmer

Evelyn Gallardo was a sales promotion whiz until her passion for primates—she fell in love with King Kong at age 3—led her to Borneo where she has spent a good portion of her life photographing orangutans in the wild.

Evelyn Gallardo has this crazy passion for things the world doesn't seem to value much. This particular Monday morning she was fighting hard for three of them:

◆ The great mountain apes of Africa — once numbered in the millions and now down to less than 30,000.

◆ Her Hispanic heritage, a culture in which children were once taught to kiss the hands of their elders and to revere nature, and now are taught only to survive.

◆ And 700 students at Braddock Drive Elementary School in Culver City — all but 16 of whom live below the poverty line and 50 percent of whom start school unable to speak English.

The combination may seem bizarre to some, but the message to the first-through-fifth-graders who packed into the school's aging auditorium that morning was simplicity itself: You have to care about yourself and each other, you have to try, and you can succeed.

To Gallardo, a 48-year-old wildlife photographer who's been featured on TV's "A Current Affair," written an award-winning children's book and who worked with gorilla researcher Dian Fossey just five months before her death — the three parts of her message are inalterably intertwined.

It's a message the Manhattan Beach resident has delivered to more than 200,000 children in 250 schools nationwide — although this is the first time she's ever personally adopted a school.

"Kids need to hear those things," she says flatly. "Even more important, they need to learn to read and to write and they need to see people like themselves who use those tools. It doesn't matter what career they choose, to achieve their dreams they're going to have to learn to read and write."

Who better to preach that particular message than a children's author, she says.

"When you write for children you need to be able to think like a child, so connecting with them is a natural."

The slender, dark-haired activist — who looks like she ought to be in front of the lens instead of behind it — does more than connect with her youthful listeners; she plays them like Itzhak Perlman with a Stradivarius.

Flicking through slides taken during her work with the giant apes in Borneo and Rwanda, she beguiles them with stories about flying snakes, squirrels and lizards, about orangutans who love to steal your bath soap — and eat it — and about poachers who kill female apes so they can steal their babies and sell them for pets.

In between each story she slips an all-but-painless bit of science: Orangutans and humans are a lot a like — about 96 percent, she tells them. "The three most important things we have in common are opposing thumbs, the ability to stand erect and large brains."

Switching to a slide of a winsome-looking female orangutan, she says, "This is Princess. She lived with a human family for awhile and learned American Sign Language, so she's bilingual like you."

She introduces them to Dr. Birute Galdikas, the German-born researcher who has spent more than 20 years in Borneo studying orangutans — and on whom Gallardo's award-winning children's book *Among the Orangutans* (Chronicle Books, $7.95) is based.

Galdikas is a primatologist, she tells them. If you like science, there are a lot of jobs you can do; there are oceanographers, biologists, astronomers...

For some the message hits home.

"I want to be a snake scientist when I grow up," says sweatshirt-clad Patricia Servin, 10, after the presentation ends. "I like watching snakes and I like the way they wind up your arm."

It's music to Santa Campuzano's ears.

After four years as principal at Braddock, the educator is grateful for every bit of motivating she can get.

"The whole idea is to get them excited about protecting and caring about life," Campuzano says candidly. "They're the ones who will be making a lot of the decisions about what happens to this planet in the future.

"And I hope that in learning to respect animals they'll also learn to love and respect each other. If they do there will be less incentive for them to join gangs."

It's a first step, she says, this learning to respect each other's differences, but it's important. "It takes all of us to make a great society."

Gallardo couldn't agree more. It was the chance to preach that particular message that drew her to this multiethnic, largely Latino campus.

"When I was a child my grandmother took me on a train to El Paso to meet my great-grandfather," she says. "It was a profound experience for me.

"He was a *curandero*, a folk healer, and he traveled with Pancho Villa. He would tell me these wonderful stories about animals, trees and plants; he helped to nurture my love of nature — my heritage has everything to do with who I am and what I do.

"The problem is the more each generation tries to assimilate the more we leave our cultural traditions behind and the values that go with them," she says. "But it doesn't have to be that way. It is possible to have one foot planted firmly in American culture and the other in one's own culture. For me culture is about connections, not separations."

Many of the school presentations Gallardo does are multicultural offerings done in tandem with fellow children's book authors Dolores Johnson, an African-American, and Janet Wong, a Chinese poet.

Gallardo, herself, has three books hanging fire. Her latest work — a picture book focusing on her Hispanic culture and traditions — is sitting on her publisher's desk, and she's just completed work on book three, the story of Davida, the orphaned orangutan that her video-producer husband David Root adopted on their first trip to Borneo.

Her fourth book — a biography of Dian Fossey — is at a standstill because of the civil unrest in Rwanda.

"We've tried to go back to do research three times," she says, "but we keep getting faxes from friends telling us journalists are being murdered there so we haven't gone."

The fact that she takes pictures and writes books for a living is still a source of amazement to her.

She was a sales promotion manager for an international Japanese firm in the early '80s when she signed up with Earth Watch — the nonprofit organization that sends volunteers to work with scientists around the world — to go do field observation on the great apes.

"I never wanted to be a photographer — I was actually afraid of cameras," she says. "But my husband was videotaping this leopard hanging from a tree one day out on the Serengeti Plains in Kenya and he shoved the still camera at me and said, 'Here, take a picture.'

"I was amazed at the results. I never knew I had any talent for photography."

Today she has an agent in New York who markets her work internationally and has had photos published in books on both Jane Goodall and Dian Fossey, as well as in textbooks, newspapers, *Science Magazine*, GEO, Zoolife, travel magazines, calendars and greeting cards.

She has photographed howler monkeys in Costa Rica, spent a month hitchhiking up the Amazon on cargo boats, dodged student riots in Peru and Colombia, a coup in Argentina and done field research on orangutans in Borneo and mountain gorillas in Rwanda.

There are, however, two things she has *not* done. She has not been to New Guinea — "it's one of the last frontiers, one of the last undiscovered places," she says — and she wants to be the first woman to photograph all four primates: gorillas, orangutans, chimpanzees and bonobos, long-limbed chimps found in the rain forests of Zaire. Two down, two to go.

Still, if she were to die today, she'd be content, she says.

"I love my life. The days are so different. I do so many things — the writing and the photography, talking about things I care about to everyone from school students to the Audobon Society, teaching — but I never imagined that so much of what I dreamed about would come true."

My Life With ORANGUTANS

A leading primatologist changes what we know about the social lives of Borneo's great red apes

Orangutangle

Orangutan study offers new insights

LEAKEY'S LAST ANGEL

MEET DR. GALDIKAS!

Motoring down a jungle river with a crew of kids and apes—it's all in a day's work for this world-famous scientist.

Orangutans in the Mist

Woman's 20-Year Study of Elusive Rain Forest Apes Finds They're Not Antisocial After All

Living With the Great Orange Apes

By BIRUTÉ M. F. GALDIKAS

Rescuer of Orangutans

Expert on apes helps popular 'pets' return to wild

Do Orangutans Remember?

Conserving the Red Ape

Persons of the Forest

Three women – a Canadian, an American, and a Briton – were handpicked by palaeontologist Louis Leakey to study the great apes as a window on early man. The Canadian, Biruté Galdikas, traded civilization for the leech-infested jungles of Borneo and a lifetime among the orang-utans

THE ORANG GANG

Birute Galdikas: The Professor of the Red Apes

BRAVING THE HELLISH JUNGLES OF BORNEO, BIRUTE GALDIKAS PROBES THE SECRETS OF ONE OF OUR OLDEST RELATIONS

information in decreasing order of importance. Be sure to include your name, the title of your book, publisher, intended audience, price, ISBN number, and contact telephone number.

When I went to Rwanda to photograph mountain gorillas for Dian Fossey in 1985, she taught me gorilla vocalizations at the dinner table each night. Knowing their language helped me earn the trust of these magnificent animals. Of course I felt a bit silly walking around the forest grunting, "Um-um-wuam, um-um-wuam," but this is how gorillas greet each other. When I communicated with them in their language—so to speak—they relaxed and allowed me to enter their world. The press release is the media's gorilla greeting. It's your introduction to *their* world. Be sure to contact your publisher before you write a press release about your book—the publicity department may already have written one. In that case ask them to send it to you so you can reproduce it.

PRESS RELEASE

Primate Productions
P.O. Box 3038
Manhattan Beach, CA 90266
Contact: David Root
Phone: 310-545-9582   For Immediate Release

AUTHOR GOES BANANAS AT BREED STREET ELEMENTARY SCHOOL!

Los Angeles—Children's author and wildlife photographer Evelyn Gallardo has gone bananas in a most unusual way. Her specialty is photographing great apes in their natural habitats. Ms. Gallardo recently returned from her third trip to Borneo and will share her adventures with Breed Street Elementary students on Friday, January 31st. She is the author of *AMONG THE ORANGUTANS* (Chronicle Books, ISBN 0-8118-0408-9), an award-winning book about Dr. Biruté Galdikas, a scientist who has studied orangutans in Borneo for nearly three decades.

Ms. Gallardo theme will be "Follow Your Dream." She will encourage Breed Street Elementary students to achieve their dreams through reading, writing, and perseverance. She will also encourage them to seek careers in science. Her fascination with apes stems from childhood, "I fell in love with King Kong. It was an early bonding experience." The author has photographed mountain gorillas in Rwanda for Dr. Dian Fossey, and orangutans in Borneo for Dr. Galdikas. Her world travels include Kenya, Nepal, Indonesia, China, India, Japan, Costa Rica, Mexico, and much of South America including the Galapagos Islands and a trip up the Amazon River. She is currently working on a picture book based on her heritage. The author studied creative writing and photography at UCLA.

###

Now, write a press release about your first school visit.

Contact:

Phone: For Immediate Release

TITLE: _____

(City)_____— Children's author _____

will _____

at (school name)_____ at (address)_____

_____ on (date and time)_____

She is the author of (book title)_____

a book about _____

_____

    Ms. (your name)_____

will (describe presentation) _____

for (school name)_____students_____

to _____and_____

Her fascination with_____ stems from _____

_____ (Your quote) "_____

_____"

    She is currently working on (describe projects)_____

and _____ The author (background)_____

_____

_____

# # #

Catalog Page

A nice touch is to follow the press release with a copy of the advertisement for your book in your publisher's catalog. If it's in color, you can add pizzazz by reproducing it. Color copiers are quite reasonably priced now. You may want to invest in one. Mine has paid for itself several times over, for having color copies made commercially is expensive. If your book shares the page with another title, cut and paste your ad onto a clean sheet of paper. Don't do as a friend of mine did and merely copy the full page. As it happened, the other author's book was advertised above hers! Whose press kit is this anyway?

Book Reviews

Add your favorable book reviews next. Your publisher will probably send you the favorable ones, but it's still a smart idea to check in via e-mail or fax periodically for new ones. Use an X-ACTO® Knife and a ruler to cut and paste your best reviews onto white paper. Cut out the title of the publication and mount it at the top of the page. Then cut out the body of the review and position it below the title. Cut close to the text for best copying results. If black cut lines still appear after you've made a copy, use liquid paper correction fluid to cover them, then duplicate the clean copy.

Adapt Your Press Kit for School, Library, and Conference Program Coordinators

This is where your press kit pulls double duty. You don't have to reinvent the wheel to get yourself hired as a speaker. Just modify your cover letter and add the following components.

Dear Author Coordinator,

It was a pleasure talking to you on the telephone today. Thank you for your interest in my author presentations. Enclosed you will find a 7-minute preview video and my press kit along with details and fees for student, educator and parent presentations. Please feel free to share the video with your colleagues. Since I have a limited number on hand, I'd appreciate it if you would return the video in the enclosed addressed envelope when you are finished with it.

My most popular presentation is "Follow Your Dream," a slide-illustrated assembly for students. For grades 3 and above, it includes amazing scientific facts, ape vocalizations, stories about my Mexican-Hopi heritage, the nonfiction writing process, careers in science and writing, audience participation, and Q & A. Grades K-2 see an abbreviated version of the slide show with a focus on storytelling and audience participation. "Follow Your Dream" is also available in Spanish or in a bilingual format.

Among the Orangutans

The Biruté Galdikas Story

BY EVELYN GALLARDO

A student of the renowned paleontologist Dr. Louis B. Leakey and a colleague of both Dian Fossey and Jane Goodall, Biruté Galdikas is the world's foremost authority on the life and behavior of the orangutan. For more than twenty years she has lived in the jungles of Borneo, devoting her life to studying and preserving this endangered animal as well as its disappearing rain forest habitat. The informative text describes both the obstacles and adventures of Dr. Galdikas's explorations as well as her startling discoveries, and the full-color photographs brilliantly capture her life among the orangutans. Biruté Galdikas is an impressive role model, and her inspiring story serves as a reminder that the future of our fragile world, as well as our understanding of it, lies in the dreams and determination of today's young naturalists.

Evelyn Gallardo is a writer, photographer, and primate enthusiast who has studied with Dr. Biruté Galdikas as well as Dr. Dian Fossey. Ms. Gallardo lives in Southern California.

The Great Naturalists Series

Each volume in this new series of natural history books introduces children to the fascinating life story of a renowned 20th-century naturalist. Complete with full-color photographs, sidebars, glossaries, and indexes, each book is an invaluable resource and a must for every home, classroom, and library.

ISBN: 0-8118-0031-8
HARDCOVER $13.95
ISBN: 0-8118-0408-9
PAPERBACK $6.95
8 BY 10 INCHES   48 PAGES
FULL-COLOR PHOTOGRAPHS
THROUGHOUT
ENGLISH-LANGUAGE RIGHTS
AGES 8 TO 12 YEARS

MARCH

Publishers Weekly

NONFICTION

★ **AMONG THE ORANGUTANS:**
The Biruté Galdikas Story
Evelyn Gallardo. Chronicle, $13.95
(48p) ISBN 0-8118-0031-8; paper $6.95
-0408-9

As orangutans slip into further endangerment due to poaching (mothers are shot in order that babies may be taken as pets) and destruction of their habitat, books such as this may inspire a backdraft of conservation. Written by a primate photographer who has accompanied Galdikas through Borneo's rainforests, this first entry in the Great Naturalists series introduces the famed primatologist and her passion. With Dian Fossey and Jane Goodall, Galdikas completes the primate research triangle whose participants were mentored by the late Louis Leakey. And like these contemporaries, Galdikas possesses remarkable determination. Orangutan research proves especially daunting: "unlike the highly social chimpanzees, great apes . . . who travel on the ground, orangutans live alone in the trees and travel by swinging." Each day, Galdikas traveled far from camp, "drenched by rain, caked with mud, and bleeding from leech bites"; she endured "mysterious infections," subsisted on canned sardines, and watched her scant belongings rot in the extreme humidity. In brief, well organized chapters and highly readable prose, Gallardo interlaces intriguing observations of orangutans with the life of their patient observer and rehabilitator. The book will rouse readers of all ages not only to a curiosity for primates, but also to admiration for those who brave adversity to eke out a larger understanding of the natural environment. Ages 8-12. *(Mar.)*

Meeting an author is often the spark that inspires even a reluctant child to read. I have recently returned from trips to Uganda and Costa Rica. I look forward to sharing my experiences with your students, educators and parents. Feel free to call me with any questions. Meanwhile, stop by my web site for a visit. The address is www.evegallardo.com.

Regards,

Evelyn Gallardo

Content Sheet

The content sheet describes your presentation in an 8½" x 11" flyer format. You can create a content sheet for each presentation or list them all on one page in a simple text form with no photos or graphics. I adapted the content sheets on the next few pages from those used by professional speakers who earn between $2,000 and $30,000 per engagement. Don't be afraid to copy the designs exactly (but not the content please!). They are professional industry standards, and after all, we are professionals.

The content sheet typically contains:

- A title in white letters on a black background, spanning the top of the page
- Benefits to the audience listed in bullet form
- Your headshot, book cover, or other relevant photo
- A brief bio
- Brief testimonial excerpts
- Contact information

Testimonial Letters

Program coordinators who've not seen your presentation will feel more comfortable hiring you when they read a glowing report from one of their colleagues. Don't expect satisfied clients to send them to you unprompted. You must solicit them. After your next performance, smile and say: "I'm updating my press kit and would love to include your candid comments. Would you be so kind as to write a few brief sentences on your (school, library or association's) letterhead? I'd really appreciate it." You must ask for the testimonial on an official letterhead, otherwise, you'll probably get a hand-written thank-you card that can't be reproduced and carries no credibility.

FOLLOW YOUR DREAM
Student Assembly

Students Explore...

√ **Amazing scientific facts**

√ **How apes communicate**

√ **How to help endangered primates**

√ **Rain forest conservation**

√ **The nonfiction writing process**

√ **How to discover their own dreams**

√ **How good writing skills can help
   them accomplish their dreams**

Also Available in Spanish

Evelyn Gallardo in Borneo

While growing up in East Los Angeles, California, Evelyn Gallardo often dreamed of traveling around the world. But her wildest dream—to visit Africa—was realized after she wrote a letter to Dr. Dian Fossey who responded with an invitation to photograph the endangered mountain gorillas of Rwanda. Another dream led Evelyn to Borneo where she was inspired to co-produce a documentary, and to write her award winning book, *AMONG THE ORANGUTANS.*

What Educators and Students Say...

"Evelyn Gallardo's visit worked on so many important levels: writing, science, conservation, geography, role model...I could go on and on! This is, I believe, precisely how to make words come alive for our students."
—Brad Rumble, Title I Coordinator, Rosemont Avenue Elementary

"Both the teachers and students agree that was by far one of the best educational programs we have ever had at our school."
—Kenneth Jacobsen, Principal, Ramona Elementary, Hawthorne

"It was a wonderful experience...a rare opportunity that got the students very interested in writing and reading and the exciting life it can offer them." —Allison McKenzie, Bathgate Elementary, Mission Viejo

"My favorite part was when she made the ape calls." —Mabeena M., 4th grader, Lunada Bay School, Palos Verdes

"What a powerful program she presents!" —Jane Hancock, Director, UCLA Young Writer's Project, Westwood

How to Create a Photo-Illustrated Book
Student Workshop

Students Benefit by...

√ **Meeting and working with an award-winning author**

√ **Hearing firsthand how to make writing come alive**

√ **Learning photography techniques from a professional photographer**

√ **Gaining exposure to careers in science, writing, and photography**

Now in its third printing, Evelyn Gallardo's book *AMONG THE ORANGUTANS* received the Nueva Award, John Burroughs Nature Book Award, the California Collection Award, and a starred review in Publisher's Weekly. Her specialty is close-up photos of great apes taken in their natural habitats. Her photography has appeared in books and on the covers of magazines around the world. She is represented by the Peter Arnold Photo Agency in New York.

Workshop Description:

Day One:

Photography the National Geographic Way

Students experience a behind-the-scenes slide show covering the creation of a nonfiction photo-illustrated book. National geographic tips, and composition are discussed in this interactive workshop. Basic camera operation and film choices are included.

Day Two:

Nonfiction in 7 Steps

This workshop includes generating unique ideas, research, organization, hooking and sustaining the reader's attention. Also covered: photo analysis, working with zoos and museums, page layout and design.

2208 The Strand, B, Manhattan Beach, CA 90266, Tel: (310) 545-9582 Fax: (310) 545-8218
EveGal@aol.com Web Site: www.evegal22@aol.com

Secrets of a Photo-Journalist
Staff Development

Educators Discover...

√ **3 National Geographic photography secrets**

√ **5 writing secrets**

√ **4 secrets for creating great titles**

√ **7 appealing page layouts and designs**

√ **25 markets for student writing**

√ **50 markets for educator writing**

Evelyn Gallardo's photographs have appeared in books, magazines, and calendars all over the world. She specializes in photographing great apes in the wild and has worked with gorilla expert Dr. Dian Fossey in Rwanda, and with orangutan authority Dr. Biruté Galdikas in Borneo. Evelyn is the author of *Among the Orangutans,* and *How to Promote Your Children's Book.* Her current writing projects include *Journey of a Wildlife Photographer*, *African Wildlife Vet*, and poetry, short stories and books based on her Mexican-Hopi heritage.

Workshop Description

In this hands-on, interactive, slide-illustrated workshop Evelyn takes participants on a behind-the-scenes peek at the creation of her award-winning book, *Among the Orangutans*. Educators learn how to compose eye-catching photographs with simple and inexpensive cameras, analyze photographs, relate text to the photographs, hook the readers attention, bring their stories full circle, and attract the reader's eye to the page. A photo session and writing exercise are included.

"The workshop exceeded my expectations! The session had an easy format to follow and understand. The writing component was equally as strong with tasks that can easily apply to a classroom setting."
—*Candy Dardarian, Harding Elementary, Sylmar, CA*

2208 The Strand, B, Manhattan Beach, CA 90266
Tel: (310) 545-9582   Fax: (310) 545-8218   e-mail: EveGal22@aol.com   Web site: www.evegallardo.com

Mexican American Culture
Staff Development & Field Study

Teacher Benefits...

√ **Earn 2 units for career increment or professional growth**

√ **Experience Southern California's rich Mexican and Spanish heritage**

√ **Explore the Presidio, Mission, and Old Town in San Diego**

√ **Expand your knowledge of Mexican American history, heroes, traditions, folklore, literature, and poetry**

√ **Discover how to create positive cultural experiences in the classroom**

Mexican-Hopi instructor Evelyn Gallardo weaves personal family tales into the historical fabric of the Mexican American experience. Her great-grandfather rode with Pancho Villa during the Mexican Revolution. He later worked as a bracero in downtown Los Angeles to help build City Hall. Evelyn is the author and contributing photographer of the award winning book, *AMONG THE ORANGUTANS*. Her upcoming picture book, *"MEETING MAMA LIPA,"* is based on a cultural tradition that she learned in childhood.

What Educators Say...

"You live the experience. Not only do you learn from the instructor, but also from the docents and fellow teachers." —Marcella Schott

One gets hands-eyes-ears-on experience. Much better than traditional classroom study." — Sarai Beato

"Evelyn Gallardo was excellent. I loved her poems and her interest in Mexican American literature." —Daniel Villalobos

"I recommend this class to my friends!" —Robert Thomas MacKenzie

"Evelyn is top notch—a real professional with charm, grace and warmth." —Sybil Goldenblank

2208 The Strand, B, Manhattan Beach, CA 90266, Tel: (310) 545-9582 Fax: (310) 545-8218
e-mail: EveGal22@aol.com Web Site: www.evegallardo.com

How to Help Your Child Create A Photo-Illustrated Book
Parent Workshop

Parents Learn About...

√ **The nonfiction writing process**

√ **3 Easy National Geographic photo techniques anyone can master**

√ **Working with zoos**

√ **Using the family album as a resource for book ideas**

√ **How good writing skills can help children succeed**

√ **Using handouts for home-use**

Evelyn Gallardo is the author-photographer of ***AMONG THE ORANGUTANS***, and co-producer of the documentary, "Orangutans: Grasping the Last Branch." She specializes in photographing great apes in the wild. She has worked with gorilla expert Dr. Dian Fossey in Rwanda, and with orangutan authority Dr. Biruté Galdikas in Borneo. Her current writing projects include poetry, short stories and picturebooks based on her Mexican-Hopi heritage.

What Parents Say...

"What a great workshop. I took my daughter to the zoo and helped her write a book about kangaroos using the family camera and one roll of film!"
—Debby Webb

"I was afraid to pick up a camera before but Evelyn Gallardo's tips gave me the confidence and know-how to help my child learn how to take photos!"
— Barbara Mollenkamp

"My son never knew what to write about until we looked through our family album and I began telling him stories about his ancestors."
—Rebecca Villanueva

2208 The Strand, B, Manhattan Beach, CA 90266
Tel: (310) 545-9582 Fax: (310) 545-8218 EveGal@aol.com Web site: www.evegallardo.com

Mysteries of the Four Great Apes
Multimedia Library Presentation

Students Explore...

√ **How apes communicate**

√ **Similarities and contrasts among the apes**

√ **Apes as humankind's closest living relatives**

√ **What draws women scientists to study apes**

√ **How to help endangered primates**

While growing up in East Los Angeles, California, Evelyn Gallardo often dreamed of traveling around the world. But her wildest dream—to visit Africa—was realized after she wrote a letter to Dr. Dian Fossey who responded with an invitation to photograph the endangered mountain gorillas of Rwanda. Another dream led Evelyn to Borneo where she was inspired to co-produce a documentary, to become a wildlife photographer, and to write her award winning book, *AMONG THE ORANGUTANS.* She is represented by the Peter Arnold Photo Agency in New York.

Description

This 60 minute slide-illustrated presentation includes video clips, ape vocalizations, amazing scientific facts, stories about the author's experiences working with apes and the women who study them, and information about careers in science, writing and photography.

What Librarians and Students are Saying...

"Evelyn Gallardo's visit worked on so many important levels: writing, science, conservation, geography, role model...I could go on and on!" —Brad Rumble, Librarian, Rosemont Avenue Elementary

"My favorite part was when she made the ape calls." —Mabeena M., 4th grader, Palos Verdes

2208 The Strand, B, Manhattan Beach, CA 90266
Tel: (310) 545-9582   Fax: (310) 545-8218   e-mail: EveGal22@aol.com   Web site: www.evegallardo.com

Now, design your own school, library or conference content sheet:

Title: _____

Students Learn...

List benefits in descending order of importance:

_____

_____

_____

_____

_____

Photo

Caption: _____

_____

Bio as it pertains to this presentation:

_____
_____
_____
_____
_____
_____
_____

What Educators and Students Say...

Testimonials (If you must, it's worth doing a free presentation to obtain them):_____

_____
_____

_____
_____
_____
_____

_____
_____
_____

Your contact information_____

Los Angeles Unified School District

Rosemont Avenue Elementary School

421 N. Rosemont Avenue, Los Angeles, CA 90026

Telephone (213) 413-5310

SIDNEY THOMPSON
Superintendent of Schools

EVARISTO BARRETT
Principal

Evelyn Gallardo
2208 The Strand, B
Manhattan Beach, CA 90266

Dear Evelyn:

On behalf of the students, parents and staff of Rosemont Avenue School, I want to thank you for sharing your talents and expertise with us. Your program was the perfect way to end this year. Here, two weeks later, students still are talking about you and our two new adoptees, Nopi and Madura. Your visit worked on so many important levels: writing, science, conservation, geography, role model...I could go on and on! And I am so pleased that your book has found its way into so many of our students' hands. This is, I believe, precisely how to make words come alive for our students.

You have a large following here in the Echo Park area awaiting your next publication. Thank you again for lighting up our June. And please do not hesitate to call on me to assist other schools who are fortunate enough to receive a visit from you.

Sincerely,

Brad Rumble
Title I Coordinator

Dear Evelyn,

I can't begin to tell you how much all of us at Bathgate enjoyed your visit. The kids were so enthusiastic and responsive to your presentation. The teachers have also continued to talk about your presentation and how much the students learned. It's a rare opportunity that the students can get so interested in writing and reading and the exciting life it can offer them. Your visit came at a perfect time also as all the grades are entering an "Earth Studies and Conservation" unit for the upcoming Open House.

Personally, I'd like to thank you for making our schools first Visiting Authors Day such a success. It was a wonderful experience to work with you. I also was so impressed with how you took the time with each student to find out about them during the book signing. I'm sure you inspired each of them.

Enclosed is one Students book that missed the signing portion of your visit. If you could personalize (the dedication is inside the book) it for her and mail it back, that would make her day.

Again, I thank you for giving our students a memorable day and really showing them what "dreaming" can do.

Sincerely,

Fee Schedule

This will probably come later down the line when you have developed more presentations. A fee schedule is a price list of each presentation you offer, such as student assemblies, staff development, parent workshops, and conference talks. It's appropriate to quote the fee in your cover letter or directly on the content sheet if you are offering only one presentation.

Optional Promotion Material

As if you didn't have enough on your plate already, I'm going to suggest some optional material you may want to develop.

Book Order Form

There are a couple of things you can do to increase your school-visit book sales. When it comes to your clients, remember this important law of the jungle: *Make their job easier by doing it for them!* If you suggest to a school author coordinator that she create an order form for your book sales, you'll find it's the rare person who makes the time and effort to do it. She has probably never seen a book order form before, doesn't have a clue where to begin, and won't have the time, energy or desire to do it anyway. Be her hero and offer to send her a ready-made master she can duplicate and distribute to every student and staff member. She'll jump at the opportunity.

I include the following letter to introduce the coordinator to her local children's bookseller and to explain the book ordering procedure.

Dear Author Coordinator,

Students, parents, and educators always appreciate the opportunity to own a personalized, autographed copy of *Among the Orangutans.* Enclosed you will find a master book order form that can be photocopied and distributed to every student and educator at your school. Ane Miller at Through a Child's Eyes bookstore in Downey handles my book sales in your area. I called the store and told Ane about our upcoming event and she looks forward to hearing from you. She can be reached at 562-806-6490.

I'm including some tips to help guide you through the simple book sales process. Of course, I'll be happy to stay until all your books are signed. Please feel free to call me with any questions. Meanwhile, stop by my web site for a visit. The address is www.evegallardo.com.

Here are a Few Easy Steps to Follow:

4-6 Weeks Before Event

- Place a minimum order of 30 books with your local children's bookseller.

- Copy the order form and distribute to teachers and students.

3 Weeks Before Event

- Pick up initial book order from bookseller.

- Distribute one book to each teacher to share with students.

2 Weeks Before Event

- Collect and count order forms.

- Order additional books from bookseller if necessary.

Day of Event

- Place completed order form in each child and educator's book.

- Have author sign books.

1 Week After Event

- Return unsold books in good condition to bookseller with a check.

Regards,

Evelyn Gallardo

Bookmark

Bookmarks can easily be designed on your computer. If your software program doesn't have a template for bookmarks, simply divide the page into columns. Design your bookmark in the first column then copy and paste it into the remaining columns. You can fit from 4-10 to a page, depending upon the size of type. Include your name, the title of your book, the publisher and the ISBN number. Consider adding the scanned cover of your book for an effective presentation. Copy the master onto card stock, and then cut. For a more festive look, punch a hole near the top and tie a short length of yarn, ribbon or raffia (straw-like material) through it.

You can design a bookmark to advertise your book at store signings, conferences, and other events. I like to send a customized bookmark master to schools a month before my visit. They can be duplicated and distributed to each student as a souvenir and a reminder of the upcoming event. It's a nifty way to remind students, parents, and educators that your book is available for purchase. Book sales don't seem quite as

Fee Schedule

Evelyn Gallardo
2208 The Strand, B
Manhattan Beach, CA 90266
(310)545-9582   (310)545-8218 Fax
E-mail: Evegal22@aol.com
Web site: www.evegallardo.com

*Fees good for
events booked
before Dec. 2000*

Student Assembly:

Follow Your Dream: 1 Large Assembly (200-300 students).................................
      Half-day: 2 Large Assemblies & 1 Class Visit...
      Full-day: 3 Large Assemblies & 1 Writing Workshop or 2 Class Visits.......

Student Writing Workshop:

How to Create a Photo-Illustrated Book: (30-60 students)
      2-Day: Two 60-90 minute sessions..
      8-Week: Eight 60-90 minute sessions...

Staff Development:

Secrets of a Photo-Journalist...
Mexican American Culture (per teacher)..

Parent Workshop:

8 Ways to Motivate Your Child to Read & Write..
How to Help Your Child Create A Photo-Illustrated Book..........................

Conference Keynote Speech: ....

Public Library Presentation:

Follow Your Dream (30-75 attendees)...
How to Create a Photo-Illustrated Book (30-75 attendees)............................
Mysteries of the Four Great Apes...

Educational Material:

Video: "Orangutans Grasping the Last Branch"...
Book: *AMONG THE ORANGUTANS*...

Payment Options:

1) 10% discount will be deducted from speaker's fee if full payment is received two (2) weeks prior to the event. Discount does not apply to travel, mileage, hotel, products or shipping.
2) 25% down upon signing of contract. Balance to be paid on the day of the event.

AUTOGRAPHED BOOK ORDER FORM

Clarence Lobo Elementary

PRESENTS

Evelyn Gallardo

Author of *AMONG THE ORANGUTANS*

Dear Parents,

Your child will meet visiting author and wildlife photographer Evelyn Gallardo *Tuesday, February 22, 2000*. Her "Follow Your Dream" presentation will include stunning photographs, storytelling, great ape vocalizations, and information about careers in writing, science and photography. Mrs. Gallardo has traveled around the world several times. She worked in Rwanda with gorilla expert Dr. Dian Fossey and in Borneo with orangutan authority Dr. Biruté Galdikas. Meeting an author often sparks even a reluctant child to read and write. Autographed books are treasured gifts. This is a wonderful opportunity to encourage your child to read!

Please order by Tuesday, February 15th, 2000

Book Title:	Price: (w/tax)	Qty:	Total:
AMONG THE ORANGUTANS	_____ x	_____ =	_____

Please make checks payable to: **Clarence Lobo Elementary**

Name(s) to be inscribed in each book: (Please print clearly)

Name_____   Name_____

Room_____   Teacher's Name_____

Now, create your own book order form:

AUTOGRAPHED BOOK ORDER FORM

School Name:

PRESENTS

Your Name:

Author of

Book Title:

Scanned
Book Jacket Photo

Dear Parents,
       Your child will meet visiting author (your name)_____
on _____ Her presentation will include _____
_____
Her book is about _____
_____ She has _____
_____
and _____
Don't miss this wonderful opportunity to encourage your child to read!

Please order by

Book Title:	**Price:**	**Qty:**	**Total:**
	(w/tax)		

_____   _____   x   _____   =   _____

Please make checks payable to: _____

Name(s) to be inscribed in each book: (Please print clearly)

       Name_____   Name_____

       Room_____   Teacher's Name_____

Bookmark

Follow Your Dream
with the author of...
Among the Orangutans

ISBN: 0-8118-0408-9

Evelyn Gallardo

will visit
Lobo Elementary
February 22, 2000

www.evegallardo.com

Follow Your Dream
with the author of...
Among the Orangutans

ISBN: 0-8118-0408-9

Evelyn Gallardo

will visit
Lobo Elementary
February 22, 2000

www.evegallardo.com

Follow Your Dream
with the author of...
Among the Orangutans

ISBN: 0-8118-0408-9

Evelyn Gallardo

will visit
Lobo Elementary
February 22, 2000

www.evegallardo.com

Follow Your Dream
with the author of...
Among the Orangutans

ISBN: 0-8118-0408-9

Evelyn Gallardo

will visit
Lobo Elementary
February 22, 2000

www.evegallardo.com

Follow Your Dream
with the author of...
Among the Orangutans

ISBN: 0-8118-0408-9

Evelyn Gallardo

will visit
Lobo Elementary
February 22, 2000

www.evegallardo.com

Follow Your Dream
with the author of...
Among the Orangutans

ISBN: 0-8118-0408-9

Evelyn Gallardo

will visit
Lobo Elementary
February 22, 2000

www.evegallardo.com

Follow Your Dream
with the author of...
Among the Orangutans

ISBN: 0-8118-0408-9

Evelyn Gallardo

will visit
Lobo Elementary
February 22, 2000

www.evegallardo.com

Follow Your Dream
with the author of...
Among the Orangutans

ISBN: 0-8118-0408-9

Evelyn Gallardo

will visit
Lobo Elementary
February 22, 2000

www.evegallardo.com

From the Writing Desk of

Evelyn Gallardo

January 14, 2000

To the Students at Clarence Lobo Elementary:

I'm excited about visiting your school and meeting you on **Tuesday, February 22nd.** Some of you may already know me from my book, ***Among the Orangutans***. I traveled to Borneo twice while writing it. If you don't know me yet, please look for my book in your library and read it!

I will first meet you in my **Follow Your Dream** assembly, where you will learn how to speak to orangutans and gorillas in *their* language, and help pick the stories I tell. Later, some of you will have the chance to work with me in a workshop, where we will write and discover how to take excellent photographs. If your parents have been invited to attend, please encourage them to come. I'd love to meet them too! Meanwhile, if you'd like to learn more about me, visit my web site at www.evegallardo.com.

Warm Wishes,

Evelyn Gallardo

Evelyn Gallardo

commercial when every child receives an autographed bookmark to commemorate the event. I had also hoped that providing an autographed bookmark would prevent kids who hadn't purchased my book from handing me crumpled bits of paper to sign. I'm sorry to report it doesn't always work. Some kids want you to sign it again with a "real" autograph. By the way, if you haven't done it already, start practicing your autograph. You may want to add some flourishes or a simple drawing that pertains to your book.

The master I send to schools is in color. I chose to incorporate the same photo I use on my "Follow Your Dream" content sheet and my "Meet the Author" label to give my material a feeling of cohesiveness, and to give students a souvenir photo from my slideshow.

Introduction Letter to Students

My friend Janet Wong, the author of several poetry books including *Good Luck Gold and Other Poems,* allowed me to shamelessly borrow this innovative and terrific idea. I know a good thing when I see it! It's a letter introducing you, the author, to students prior to a school visit. Whereas Janet's letter was simple text, I added graphics to make it look like a page out of my personal notebook. Kids and author coordinators love it. The letter can be photocopied for each student, reproduced for each classroom and posted on its bulletin board, copied in the school newsletter, or read over the school's public address system. Students feel special that you've written to them, it reminds them to read your book before you arrive, and it empowers the idea of inviting book-buying parents to your presentation.

In Conclusion

Remember, your promotion material reflects on you as a professional. Study my material and that of other authors. Don't just copy what you see. Be creative, innovative, and let your imagination soar. Don't be afraid to add a little razzle-dazzle, a sprinkling of pizzazz. The idea is not to be exactly like everyone else but to develop your own style, one that sets you apart from the crowd. Your material can be whimsical, childlike or straightforward. Test it before you mass-produce it. If something isn't getting results, analyze it and ask yourself how you can improve it. Show it to your colleagues and ask their opinion. I'm still striving to improve the quality of my material and I constantly seek out new ideas.

Chapter Four

Bush Tactics

How to Attract the Media

You wouldn't go into Borneo to photograph orangutans without first preparing an expedition plan. You'd plan your itinerary, chart your journey on a good map, master enough of the lingo to impress the natives, learn a bit about the customs so as not to commit any major faux päs, and you'd pack the right gear so as not to get caught in a downpour without a raincoat.

So before you start beating your tom-toms to attract the media, you'll want to come up with a carefully laid plan.

Your media expedition plan will include:

- Assembling a press kit
- Compiling a media list
- Contacting the media
- Getting your first press clipping
- Attracting bigger game

Knowing what the media consider to be "news" is helpful. The initial release of your book is news. Winning an award is news. Both of these angles work especially well for your neighborhood paper. Your success reflects favorably on the community and makes everyone feel good. With the right hook, speaking at the library, a school, or to a community group can also be considered news.

Dovetailing is another way of getting into print. This means tying your book to a related story or current event. For instance, when the evening news ran the story about U.S. student science scores being among the worst in the world, I sent out a press release inviting the media to a school I was visiting. I made reference to the data in the release, then focused on what this children's author was doing to get students excited about science. Since my book is a biography about a scientist, it was a perfect tie-in. A local reporter came out and covered the story. Every year around Earth Day I send out press releases as well. The point is to keep your nose to the wind for news and events that relate to your book.

In the past fourteen years, thirty-three articles have been written about me, primarily in newspapers. My secret: I generated 90% of them. I wrote two, personal friends wrote three, author coordinators at schools initiated five others after I put a bug in their ear, and the rest came about through press releases. Not once did anyone knock on my door and ask, "Can I write a story about you?" The following bush tactics served me well.

Bush Tactic #1- Do Their Job for Them

Media people are busy. Deadlines tug at their cuffs like quicksand. The easier you make their job, the more likely they are to cover your story. Answer the following questions to help you create media-friendly material that clearly and concisely tell them who you are, what your book is about, who will want to read it, and why they should write the story.

Who is my audience? _____

_____

What makes my book or me newsworthy? _____

_____

What makes my book stand out from the competition? _____

_____

Which events, holidays, or seasons tie in with my book? _____

_____

Bush Tactic #2 – Polish Your Gear: The Press Kit

You drafted your press kit in Chapter Three. Now is the time to polish each component. Is each piece clear, concise, and inviting to the eye? Did you leave enough white space? Do any of the components look cluttered? Are the copies clean? Does the total package help the media understand your story?

Your first press kit will probably be a simple one and include a cover letter, your bio, a press release, and a copy of your book. Depending on the number of promotional copies your publisher provides, it may not be possible to send a copy to everyone on your media list. Remember to make your list available to your publisher. You don't want duplicate efforts.

I prefer a more complete kit and include copies of book reviews, a black-and-white glossy headshot, brochure, and a business card. Mine costs about $1.25 to produce in color. I saved money by purchasing my own color copy machine—the quality and affordability have improved tremendously.

The media are so inundated with press kits that I try to make mine stand out from the crowd. The human eye is attracted to warm colors such as yellow, red and orange. If your book cover incorporates a warm color, select a coordinating two-pocket folder. Your press kit will be conspicuous on any reporter's desk.

Bush Tactic #3 - Compile a Media List

Before leaving home to photograph apes in the wild, I always make a list of the specific shots I hope to get. If I run through the forest clicking the shutter at anything that moves, I may get lucky, but chances are the results will be disappointing.

The same is true with the media. You need to focus your list, know what you want—then go for it.

A good media list has three categories:
- A-List: Priority
- B-List: Desirable
- C-List: Long shots

The A-List: Media Most Likely to Cover Your Story

To get started on your A-List, think about your personal contacts. Do you have family, friends, colleagues or acquaintances on staff with newspapers, magazines, newsletters or other media? Ask everyone you know for names of media contacts, however remote they may seem. Does your sister's neighbor's daughter work for a newspaper? Look through all those business cards you collected at conferences, writing classes and social events. You can then compile the rest of your list by going to your local library and looking through Bacon's Radio & Television Directory at the reference desk.

Begin compiling your A-List in the spaces below.

List the names of three personal contacts.

_____

_____

_____

What is the name and phone number of your local newspaper?

_____

Who handles its local authors?

_____

List three regional newspapers.

_____

_____

_____

What is the name and number of your city's largest newspaper?

_____

What is the name and number of your local cable television station?

_____

List three local radio stations.

_____

_____

_____

What is the phone and contact person in your area for National Public Radio (NPR)?

_____

List three regional magazines related to your book's topic.

_____

_____

_____

List three newsletters related to your topic.

_____

_____

_____

B-List: Desirable But Not as Likely to Bite

The media on your B-List are worth contacting. It would be a coup to get coverage from them—just realize that they're a bit of a long shot.

List two local morning television talk shows.

_____

_____

List three local independent television stations.

_____

_____

_____

List two national trade magazines related to your book's topic.

_____

_____

List two syndicated radio shows.

_____

_____

C-List: Probably-Won't-Get-Them-in-a-Gazillion-Years

Don't expect Oprah to speed-dial you from her limo. But if you want to shoot for the moon, who's to stop you from trying? Go for it. Persistence is a miraculous thing.

- People Magazine
- Oprah Winfrey
- National television news
- National talk shows

Bush Tactic #4 - Get Your First Press Clipping

An effective media-luring tactic is to convince your neighborhood paper to run a story about you. Local papers are often free and unflatteringly referred to as "throwaways." But don't throw away this opportunity. It's a critical stepping-stone.

Your neighborhood paper doesn't report on international news. Its job is to cover local events and people. That's you. It's your job as an author to let the paper know about your book. In your cover letter introduce yourself as a local resident, write a press release, and always include a copy of your book in your press kit. This is the publication most likely to do a story, and omitting your book will make you look like Scrooge.

In the unlikely case that you don't drum up immediate interest, create an event and invite the reporter. Events can include—but are not limited to—a library presentation, a local school visit, a publication party or a talk to a community group. Do it for free if you have to—but give the reporter something to write about!

Bush Tactic #5 - Contact the Media

Begin by calling each media office and asking for the name and title of the person who handles stories about local authors. In some cases it will be an editor, in others it will be a reporter. Addressing your mail to a specific person will insure that the package gets opened and at least skimmed—as opposed to sitting in a "slush" pile. Make time to read an issue of the paper/magazine/newsletter, listen to the radio program or watch the television show. Then customize your cover letter with one or two sentences that mention an interesting detail.

One week after your mailing, call your contact person. When you get through, first confirm that your material was received. If not, then you really don't have much to talk about. Put a duplicate package in the mail and call back in another week. If your material was received, mention that you'll only take a few moments and ask if it's a good time to talk. If she's clearly up to her armpits in alligators, make an appointment to call back. Don't expect to get through to the right person immediately. Keep trying and don't be discouraged.

The Telephone Pitch

A good telephone pitch will entice the media to write about you and your book. *How to Get Your Point Across in 30 Seconds or Less,* by Milo O. Foreman, is an excellent resource to help you tighten your spiel. Remember, reporters are busy people and they appreciate brevity on the phone. Make your pitch two minutes or less. Write it out word for word and practice out loud. Once you know it, write one-word cues on an index card to make your delivery sound more natural. Be enthusiastic. If you don't sound excited about your book you can't expect anyone else to be wild about it either. Here's the pitch I used with my local paper.

"Hello. This is Evelyn Gallardo. I'm a local resident of Manhattan Beach and I have a new book out, *Among the Orangutans*. Did you receive the copy I sent you? Terrific! I know you're busy. I promise to be brief. Do you have two minutes to talk? Wonderful! I'm really excited about this book. It's about a woman scientist who has been studying orangutans and preserving their rain forest habitat in Borneo for nearly three decades. What makes it different is that I traveled to Borneo twice, worked with the orangutans myself, and took many of the photos."

"I really agree with the piece you wrote last week about recycling in our schools--children can and do make a powerful impact on the environment. Your readers might be interested in my education program. It makes students aware of orangutans as an endangered species, and gives them information and tools to help save the apes and their habitat. I have a couple of school visits coming up. I'd love to invite you to one. Otherwise, we can meet at your convenience. Is this the kind of story you think your readers might appreciate?"

Notice that by placing emphasis on the reporter's readers, students, and the education program, my pitch sounded less like self-promotion and more like a community service. If your contact wants to write the story, she will ask to set up an appointment for an interview. Whatever the outcome, don't take it personally, and don't behave like a Tasmanian devil if she decides to pass. You want to nurture a relationship, not spray it with repellent. There will be other reasons to contact her in the future.

Now, write your own two-minute pitch.

"Hi. My name is _____

I've been a local resident of _____ for _____

I have a new book out called _____

It's about _____

_____

It's written for _____ What makes it different is _____

_____

I'm really excited about it because _____

_____

I think your readers would be interested in it because _____

I really enjoyed reading your recent article about _____

_____

_____

I'd like to send you a copy of my book. Shall I mark it to your attention? Terrific. By the way, I'll be appearing at _____ on _____ at (time) _____ I'll include a press release and would love it if you could be there.

Meanwhile, if you agree that your readers will find my book of interest, I'm available for interviews. Thank you for _____ I look forward to _____

The Interview

As soon as you make an appointment for an interview, start preparing for it. Again, refer to *How to Get Your Point Across in 30 Seconds or Less*. Know what you want to say and how you want to say it. Jot down your three main points. There are techniques for making your point—no matter what you're asked. I'll cover those in the following section.

Follow-up with a thank-you note after *every* media interview. This is critical. Writers often like to cover new angles on past stories. One L.A. Times reporter wrote three articles about me in two years. If you don't have the courtesy to say thank you, the reporter may not remember you when you call about your next book. Verne Palmer, a reporter for the Daily Breeze, contacted me three years after she received a press release from a columnist who had done a story on me. Verne had filed it away and forgotten it. The day she called me she was digging through her files looking for a story about multiculturalism. Did I have a multicultural angle she could cover? Luckily, I had a school visit coming up at Braddock Drive Elementary, a local school I had adopted.

"Can you give me a day?" I said. "I might have something for you."

I called Dolores Johnson, the author and illustrator of several books including *Papa's Stories*, and asked if she would mind doing a "freebie" with me at a school where the press would be attending. One Latina author plus one African American author equals a multicultural event.

After Verne covered the event and wrote an exceptionally glowing piece, I sent her a thank-you card and enclosed a $500 Indonesian rupiah bill with a picture of an orangutan on it. I warned her not to get too excited—it was only worth 25 cents.

Bush Tactic #6 - Attract Bigger Game

After you bag your first press clipping, you can use it to attract bigger game. Feature it prominently in the press kits you send to others on your A-List. When you get another story move on to your B-List, etc.

Once someone in the media finds you newsworthy, others are likely to follow. It's the nature of the beast. Now that we've covered the print media extensively, let's move on to electronic media.

Radio

The beauty of radio is that you can sit at home in your bathrobe and reach literally millions of listeners around the country. Good preparation makes for a good interview. Know as much about the topic of your book as possible—even aspects that are remotely related. Here again, prior to the interview, decide on three important points you plan to make.

During the interview avoid dry answers. Respond to questions in an upbeat manner. Emphasize the positive even if the question is a negative one. Make your three points without fail, using the following bridging techniques.

Bridging phrases:

- "That's true, and another important point is that..."
- "That may be so, but what people really need to know is..."
- "Well, I don't know about that but what I do know is this..."
- "Perhaps, but I think the real question here is…"

For example, in one radio interview my three points were: to make the audience aware that orangutans are critically endangered, to let them know how they could help, and to mention the Orangutan Foundation International's toll free number. When the interviewer asked, "Aren't orangutans big, hairy beasts—have you ever been attacked by one?" I answered, "No. Their nature is shy and gentle. It's one reason they're so critically endangered. They'd rather flee than confront poachers." When asked what was the main threat to orangutans, I answered, "Rain forest devastation. When people ask me how they can help, I suggest they call 1-800-ORANGUTAN for information about replanting trees in the Borneo forest."

Television

Cable television is your best bet. Your local station will likely have someone with a show who is willing to interview an author. Call and ask for contact information. Sometimes I include, along with my press kit, a list of questions that I'd like to be asked. Some interviewers find it helpful others ignore it.

Once you nail down the interview—allow plenty of time to prepare. The more prepared you are, the less nervous you'll be. I write cue words on an index card then put the card on the floor after checking with the camera operator to make sure it's out of range.

TV tips:

- Arrive early.

- Bring two copies of your book for on-camera shots.

- Look at the host, not the camera.

- Lean slightly toward the host, with confident body language.

- Keep your hands off the microphone clipped to your clothes.

- Don't wear black or white. Red tends to bleed on camera.

- Don't wear dots or thin stripes; they vibrate and dance on camera.

- Bring two blank VHS tapes and request copies of the interview.

Keep one tape as a master to make copies as you need them. Send copies of the interview along with your press kit to your independent television stations and local morning talk shows.

Radio-TV Interview Report

In addition to sending out press kits and releases, you might consider advertising in Radio-TV Interview Report. Everyone who books guests for radio and TV talk shows uses this publication as a resource. However, I offer an important caveat—traditionally children's authors don't do well here. I only mention it because it was mildly successful for me and the media contacts I made asked me to call for another interview when my next book comes out.

> Bradley Communications
> Radio-TV Interview Report
> 135 E. Plumstead Avenue
> Lansdowne, PA 19050-8206
> 800-989-1400

If you have a hook that will appeal to the media, and if you have a few hundred dollars lying around, you may want to give it a shot. In 1993 when I placed half-page ads in three issues for a total of $696, I got fourteen radio and three cable television interviews. I then maximized my exposure by calling bookstores in

RADIO-TV
INTERVIEW REPORT
The Magazine to Read for Guests & Ideas

Do a Show on the Mysterious Dr. Birute' Galdikas and Her Life Among the Orangutans in Borneo

Evelyn Gallardo, primate photographer and author of *AMONG THE ORANGUTANS*, ascended into the dark depths of the rainforests to record the undaunting determination of Birute' Galdikas. With camera and pen she followed as Galdikas traveled far from camp, "drenched by rain, caked with mud, and bleeding from leech bites." Birute', a student of renowned paleontologist Dr. Louis Leakey and colleague of both Dian Fossey and Jane Goodall, endured "mysterious in-

At Camp Leaky in Borneo former pet orangutans often caught human taxi rides from author Evelyn Gallardo

fections," subsisted on canned sardines, and watched her scant belongings rot in the extreme humidity. The doctor had been living like this for *twenty-three years.* Why?

Gallardo will answer that question as she gives your audience a fascinating glimpse of the solitary and unbelievable life of a true environmentalist. They'll hear the incredible story of a woman devoted to the study of primates and her day-to-day struggles and triumphs. Gallardo's narrative will take listeners into the remote jungle where Dr. Galdikas sits among the great red apes taking on the roles of interpreter, teacher, friend and mother. They'll feel her frustrations as she tries to delicately balance her work, marriage and family in an unexplored territory.

Evelyn Gallardo will lead your audience on an unforgettable journey through the untamed rainforests as seen through the eyes of one of the most devoted naturalists of this century.

AVAILABILITY: Nationwide by arrangement and via telephone
CONTACT: Evelyn Gallardo, (310) 545-9582 (CA)

48

the cities where the interviews took place to make them aware of the upcoming exposure. Most thanked me for notifying them and promised to order copies of my book.

Should You Hire a Publicist?

Simply stated, publicists get your name in the news whether it's in print, radio or television. They help determine publicity campaign goals and strategies. They develop promotional materials and pitches, and they fulfill media requests for interviews with their clients. Monthly retainers typically run from $2,000-$25,000.

Publicists work best for authors with track records and several published books. Hiring one is a major investment with no guarantee of tangible results. If you'd like to learn some of the tricks of the trade without spending the big bucks, I recommend reading the following books.

Guerrilla P.R.—How You Can Wage an Effective
Publicity Campaign without Going Broke
Michael Levine, HarperCollins

Book Blitz—Getting Your Book in the News
Barbara Gaughen, Best-Seller Books

Perpetual Promotion—How to Contact Producers
and Create Media Appearances for Book Promotion
Brian Jud, Marketing Directions, Inc.

In Conclusion

You don't need a publicist to get publicity. Once you figure out what's different and newsworthy about you and your book, you'll be able to plan and organize your own publicity campaign. Contrary to what you may have thought, you are in charge of your interviews. Focus on your main points and use bridging phrases to get them across.

The media eat up stories about kids—which puts you in a perfect position. You may not get on CNN, but with the right promotional tools and just a bit of courage, your media expedition will lead you into print, onto local radio and cable television. After that—who knows?

Chapter Five

Go Ape!
The Publication Party

Surely you must have dreamed about this night during all those days, weeks, and years you sweated over your manuscript. Go ahead—go ape—swing through the trees, beat your chest and let out a Tarzan yell. Your book is now something that you, your family, friends and colleagues can see, touch and even smell. Under no circumstances deny yourself the fulfillment and heady pleasure of the publication party. This is your official literary debut. It's your night to shine.

Location

The first thing to do is decide on a location. Will it be at a bookstore, your home or the home of a friend? I recommend pitching your local bookstore to host the event. It's good public relations—the bookseller will appreciate the business and the new customers it will attract, and she will continue to promote your book long after the party is over. Drop by the store and propose the party in person. Mention how many guests you plan to invite. Children's bookstores are ideal locations for this type of event. Contact the Association of Booksellers for Children (ABC) for information about its member stores across the nation.

ABC National Office

4412 Chowen Ave. So. #303

Minneapolis, MN 55410

800-421-1665

e-mail: ccabc@vsi.com, Web site: www.abcf.com

If you have the publication party at a private home you'll have to supply the books, handle the money, keep track of the inventory, provide snacks, and help clean up afterward. You will also exclude the public from "dropping in" to see what the hoopla is about.

The Invitation

You can buy party invitations or create your own. Consider scanning your book cover and designing postcard or greeting card invitations on your computer. Remember to get the artist's permission if you don't own the copyright. Many software programs have templates for cards. You can make quality color invitations right at home. Although it won't be as classy, another alternative is to design a flyer that converts into a mailer.

Compile your Mailing List

Family, friends, colleagues, media, former teachers, acquaintances, and everyone you know, ever have known or ever hope to know should be invited. Besides helping you celebrate the publication of your book you'll need their support as book buyers. Each person who walks out with a signed copy of your book will become your champion, advocate, and village crier. More about that later.

Send out Press Releases

Let everyone on your A-List know about your publication party. It's a social event and someone might cover it. A local reporter may have kids and want to bring them along. It's worth a shot.

Refreshments

Don't expect your bookseller host to provide refreshments unless the store already has a food concession. But do discuss providing them yourself. My friend Janet Wong provided dim sum at a party for her book *Good Luck Gold and Other Poems,* which includes poems about her Chinese heritage. The bookseller brought tea and cookies. Add atmosphere to your party by coming up with creative appetizers that somehow tie in with your book.

The Program

Having a publication party means more than just showing up to autograph your books. People will expect you to do a short reading and acknowledge those who helped or supported you. Remember to request a call to action. These are your strongest supporters who want to see you and your book succeed. Ask them to spread the word. The "formal" presentation is 10-20 minutes.

Fill in the blanks below to help you prepare for your big night.

Welcoming remarks: _____

_____

_____

How did my book come about? _____

_____

_____

Who do I want to acknowledge and how did they contribute? _____

_____

_____

_____

_____

_____

What passage will I read from my book? (Read the entire text if it's a picture book.) _____

_____

_____

What is the bookseller's name and how do I wish to acknowledge her? _____

_____

_____

Write a brief pitch for the store. _____

_____

_____

How do I want to approach people about spreading the word about my book? _____

_____

_____

Concluding remarks: _____

_____

_____

What to Wear

Wear something fun, creative or elegant to your publication party. If you can come up with a costume related to your book—all the better. I wore a safari suit for mine. For my next book I'll wear something flowing and elegant. Arriving in a tee-shirt and jeans isn't very festive and it certainly won't help drop-ins at the bookstore figure out that you are the esteemed author.

Autographing Books

Give this some serious thought prior to your event. Writing "best wishes" on everyone's book is boring. Consider who will be there and think of special messages you might write to good friends and family. You're a writer and they will expect at least a bit of eloquence. Then come up with three or four phrases that will suit everyone else. For instance, I wrote: "Go ape!" "Follow your dream," and "Hang in there!" Add the date, and if you're artistic, draw a quick picture, as it adds to the book's value. If you're embarrassed by your stick figures like I am, a fun alternative is to stop in at a stamp store—they're cropping up everywhere—and find a stamp that reflects your book. Buy a colorful inkpad to go with it and put a stamp under your signature in each person's book. One caution though, don't close the cover right away as the ink doesn't dry immediately. I've found that placing a Post-it® Note over the stamp keeps it from smearing.

A Souvenir

Consider sending everyone home with an inexpensive souvenir such as a bookmark or postcard to commemorate the special event. Choose an item they can take several of to pass along to friends and family members who might be interested in your book. Design and produce the party favor yourself for a sentimental and personal touch.

In Conclusion

Have a friend take photographs. If no one from the media covers the event, send a couple of captioned photos to your neighborhood paper with a short piece written in the third person. Just leave out the by-line.

Be sure to sign a book for your host and offer to autograph any copies that are left over. There will be people who didn't make it to the party who will drop by the store wanting a copy later. Even if the bookseller returns unsold copies to the publisher, no one will object to the bonus of the author's autograph. However, do not date these copies. A six-month-old autograph is not appealing to most people. Send a thank-you note to the bookseller—and do it promptly.

Chapter Six

On Safari
The Book Store Expedition

There's nothing like your first safari. You wake up, pull back the flap of your tent, and peer out over the vast savannah. You feel exhilarated, daring, and fearful—all at the same time.

Whether you're on the Serengeti Plains of Tanzania or standing in the parking lot outside your very first bookstore—the feelings of trepidation are the same. You're about to explore unknown territory. The hairs at the nape of your neck begin to bristle.

The first time I walked into a bookstore to introduce myself as an author, I felt like a bloodsucking leech slithering through the shelves, thinking, *they'll think I'm pushy, this is a bad time, the owner's too busy.* Frankly, I dislike meeting new people. My idea of mingling at social gatherings is to avoid eye contact and leave early. In this case, I not only slipped out without saying a word, I said nothing at the next store either.

Finally, at the third store, I got up the nerve to actually open my mouth. I was shocked. The owner was happy to meet me! He smiled, shook my hand enthusiastically, and thanked me for coming: "What a pleasant break in my day. I've been dealing with cranky customers, leaky roofs, and paperwork."

Booksellers really do want to meet you. So venture out from behind your trusty computer and set out on your first bookseller safari. I've been to more than 100 bookstores from Seattle to San Diego, from New York to Los Angeles. I'll be your "bwana" and guide you every step of the way.

Independent Book Stores

Independent bookstores are on the threatened species list. Individuals who strive to provide books and services that fit the needs of their communities own them. Children's bookstores are independents. If you live in a large city, chances are there will be one in your area. Check the Yellow Pages for the store nearest you. We'll discuss chain stores later.

Call or Drop In?

Booksellers usually prefer that you phone ahead for an appointment. Grab the yellow pages and make a few calls. But is it ever all right just to drop in? I do it all the time. Since my first terrifying experience I've developed a Pavlovian response to stores that catch my eye. The secret to "dropping in" is to avoid busy times such as opening, closing, lunch, after school hours or weekends. Pick a slow time such as mid-morning or mid-afternoon. When you first start out, call ahead. It will be easier on your nerves if you're expected.

Children's bookstores are the ideal place to begin. If there aren't any near you, pick a store with an extensive children's section.

The Two-Minute Pitch

It's important to realize that booksellers are busy. Respect their time. The most effective approach I've found is the two-minute pitch. Like a picture book, it's short, descriptive and memorable.

Here's My Two-minute Pitch:

"Hi. I know you're a busy person and I'll only take two minutes of your time. I just wanted to stop by to introduce myself. I'm your local children's author, Evelyn Gallardo, and I'm here to help you sell my new book, *Among the Orangutans*." (I then hand a copy of my book to the bookseller as if it were a precious artifact sought by Indiana Jones.)

"It's published by Chronicle and it's a biography about Dr. Biruté Galdikas, the scientist who's been studying orangutans in Borneo for over 26 years. She's the Jane Goodall of the red apes. It's written for 8-12 year-olds and it got a starred review in Publisher's Weekly. Here's a copy of the review for you to keep."

"I'm available for promotional events such as book signings, community events, school visits, parent workshops and staff development. Please feel free to pass along my brochures to local educators who come into your store. If they hire me at their schools, I'd love for you to handle my books sales. Here's my business card and some extra brochures."

To prepare your pitch, answer these questions:

1. Who am I, and what are my qualifications for writing this book? _____

_____

2. What is my book about? _____

_____

3. Who is my target audience? _____

4. What type of events am I willing to do? _____

_____

5. When am I available? _____

Now, polish your pitch and practice it. Once you know you it, you'll want to prepare some material for your presentation. Never go into a store empty-handed. The bookseller may not have your book in stock.

Arm yourself with these promotional tools:

- A copy of your book
- Copies of a good review
- Brochures
- Business cards

Now you're ready to meet your first bookseller. Arrive early and browse through the store. Approach the bookseller with a smile, make direct eye contact, introduce yourself with a firm handshake, and then deliver your pitch with enthusiasm. After your dazzling dialogue, flash your best smile and let the bookseller speak. Of course, if she has something to say during your pitch, don't go on like a chattering monkey. Stop, listen, comment, and then continue on.

If the bookseller does not recognize your book, she'll check her inventory to see if she has it in stock. If so, offer to autograph it. Then ask, "Do you have a special place where you display autographed books?" Sometimes that place is right behind the cash register. Suddenly your book will be on prominent display. If she doesn't have your book on hand, offer to return and autograph any copies that she orders.

Now steer the conversation toward promotional events. If the bookseller has not had much luck with author signings, she may be reluctant to suggest one. Don't push it. When no one shows up for a book signing, it's embarrassing for the bookseller and the author. Trust the bookseller on this one. Instead ask about other possible events.

Follow-up questions:

1. What kind of promotional events do you do?
2. Do you have in-store workshops?
3. Do you do staff development for teachers?
4. Do you recommend authors for school visits?
5. Do you participate in an authors' fair?
6. Do you do book talks?
7. Do you do book fairs?
8. Are you participating in any upcoming local conferences?
9. Do you participate in local book festivals?
10. In which community events do you participate?

All of these are viable venues. Be sure to have your calendar handy just in case there's an upcoming event in which you might participate.

One note of caution: If you walk into a store without an appointment and things seem hectic or distressed, come back another day.

You'll want to understand what happens at events in which bookstores are likely to participate. Some of these may sound similar, but each one is distinct.

Book Signings

When a bookseller is gracious enough to host a signing for you, you'll need to do much more than simply arrive at the appointed hour. It's your job to help make the event successful. When a book signing flops—the bookseller feels badly too. She wants the event to be a success. Have a candid discussion with her beforehand.

Ask these questions:

1. How will this event be promoted?
2. Which newspapers will you notify?
3. Do you have a newsletter, and if so, will the event be included?
4. Will there be a poster?
5. Do you plan to hand out flyers to your customers?
6. How can we get local teachers and PTA members to attend?

After you determine what the bookseller is willing to do, enthusiastically enhance her efforts with your own.

To promote your book signing, consider the following:

1. Send press releases to the media not on the bookseller's list.
2. Ask friends in the area to bring guests and spread the word.
3. Provide a poster if the store doesn't make one.
4. Provide the bookseller with a window display.
5. Design a bookmark and leave copies with the store.
6. Post flyers in local businesses.
7. Send invitations to people on your mailing list, or offer to provide the bookseller with preprinted mailing labels.

A successful event requires time and preparation. Call media not being contacted by the bookseller and ask how far in advance they prefer to receive their press releases. Don't send them earlier or later than suggested—they'll only end up in the round file. Send out your personal mailing three to four weeks in advance. Follow up by calling friends a few days before the event as a reminder. If you provide the bookseller with a poster or a window display be sure to get it to the store at least two weeks in advance. Distribute flyers two weeks ahead.

On the day of the signing—don't just sit there! Attract people to your table. I target parents with children. First I make direct eye contact, then I smile, lean forward in my chair, stretch out my hand and say, "Hi! I'm Evelyn Gallardo. I'm your local children's author. I don't get out from behind my computer very often. Why don't you bring your kids on over to meet me?" Then I smile at the kids, "Have you ever met a real author before? Would you like a peek at my book?" I know of one enterprising writer who lures customers to her table with free samples of chocolate. Through trial and error you'll come up with an enticement that works for you.

Through a Child's Eyes bookstore owner Ane Miller says, "Providing an activity is especially important with new authors. It creates an extra incentive that helps attract an audience." Some of her well-attended book signings have included a piñata party, and a presentation creating wearable cut-out crafts related to the book's main character. If you're artistic, consider designing a make-and-take craft. Joan Bransfield Graham, the author of *Splish Splash*, a book of water poems, teaches children how to make colorful fish magnets. Her new poetry book, *Flicker Flash*, celebrates the many forms of light, from the flicker of birthday candles to the flash of lightening. To get kids involved, she invites seven children to don star crowns and form the shape of the big dipper. Sometimes I have kids make monkeys with moveable parts. They cut out the pattern on construction paper, and then attach the arms, legs and tail with clasps. Alexis O'Neill is the author of *Loud Emily*, a book about a girl who runs away and joins the crew of a whaling ship. Alexis involves her audience by having them join her in singing a rousing Irish sea chantey. The operative phrase here is "involve your audience." Don't be a talking head. Read from your book, do a storytelling session, or lead a discussion, but do something fun, creative, and interactive.

When possible, I do a preview of my slide show, especially if teachers and parents are expected. This doesn't require an elaborate set up. In one small store a children's bookseller made a screen by hanging butcher paper from a shelf, and draped sheets over the front windows to block the light. I projected my slides from a tiny table by the cash register. Thirty people showed up and as a result I was booked at five local schools. Four of them asked the bookseller to handle their book sales. People feel more comfortable recommending you at their schools if they can preview your presentation.

After the signing, offer to autograph any unsold books. Be sure to thank your host and the staff, and then follow up in writing.

Workshops

Some authors offer in-store writing workshops. It's best to get R.S.V.P.s for this type of event to be assured that there will be enough participants. Sometimes there is a small fee that the bookseller may pass on to you. The workshops can be for children, the general public, or for educators.

Staff Development

Some booksellers conduct classes for educators at the school site. The topics vary widely and may include multicultural literature, early literacy, and integrating children's literature into the curriculum. Even if the bookseller doesn't invite you to participate, you can ask her to recommend your book or your services.

School Visits

When a bookseller handles book sales for a school appearance, she generally does not attend the event. Her role is to provide your books in a timely manner. This is done through the school's author coordinator. The coordinator estimates the number of books that will be sold then calls in the order. It is usually her responsibility to pick up the books prior to the event, return any unsold copies after the event, and to pay the bookseller.

Some authors prefer to sell their own books and make an additional profit beyond the performance fee. But many booksellers view this as competition, making them less inclined to promote these authors' books and services.

My preference is to nurture symbiotic relationships. Booksellers recommend my book and my services, and in turn I ask them to handle sales for my events and send people to their stores. I really don't like making change and taking checks when I'm trying to autograph books. I might lose some short-term money, but I gain a long-term relationship with a retailer who will look forward to my next book.

Conferences

Booksellers often set up booths at conferences and trade shows. If you know of someone who is participating in such an event, offer to sign books at her booth. You can often find conference information online that includes a list of vendors.

Book Fairs

A book fair is a school event that takes place over several days. Books are laid out for display and children and parents are encouraged to purchase them. There are publishing companies such as Scholastic that run book fairs, and some booksellers conduct them as well. Ask the bookseller to include your books and offer to autograph them at the event. On occasion, authors are hired to perform at these functions, but the pay is generally nominal.

Book Festivals

Book festivals are community literary events that often take place outdoors. A variety of vendors set up displays, including booksellers, libraries, and nonprofit organizations.

One of the most successful ones I've participated in is the Los Angeles Times Festival of Books, first held in 1996 at UCLA. The organizers estimated 40,000 people would attend the weekend event. That many showed up the first day alone, with a two-day attendance of more than 75,000. In 1999, more than 100,000 came to see storytellers, magicians, musicians, costumed television characters, artists, and authors. The authors who gave presentations or participated on panels signed their books. Even if you aren't on the program, you can call participating booksellers and offer to do a book signing at their booth. Call the festival organizers, tell them you're an author, and ask for a copy of the vendor list.

How to Approach Chain Stores

Chain stores operate differently from the independents. Chains such as Barnes & Noble or Borders have a Community Relations Coordinator (CRC) in each store who books that store's events. The CRC reports to a District Community Relations Manager and this is the person you need to contact to get into multiple stores. Call the local store for information.

A CRC for Barnes & Noble suggests, "Your initial contact should be by phone. Call and offer to send your press kit. We like to look over your materials first." She also suggests sending a copy of your book if the store doesn't have one. If you can't do that, then send the book jacket including a couple of segments from the text. She cautions, "Don't just assume that because you have a book we'll arrange a signing."

A week after sending out your materials, make a follow-up call. If the CRC or the Manager is interested, she'll let you know. If you're booked for an event, she'll create an in-store poster, flyers, and send an announcement to the calendar section of the newspaper. Whether the paper picks it up or not is uncertain. Most papers work with limited space.

A Barnes & Noble is more likely to book you into an existing event such as Storytime, Book Club, or American Girls (for ages 8-12), where they already have an established audience. When I did a signing at a B & N in Long Beach, they brought in a class of 7th-graders who walked over from their school a few blocks away. Of course, I didn't get paid for the event—only professional clowns, puppeteers, etc., can charge for in-store events—but I did pass along a press kit to the teacher and pitched him for a school visit.

Chain stores also participate in book festivals and other community events. Ask about these and offer to sign at their booth.

In Conclusion

One way to make bookstore signings profitable is to have plenty of brochures on hand to promote your services at schools, libraries and conferences. If you're doing a presentation, announce your availability for school visits at the end of your talk and invite teachers, PTA members, and librarians to ask for details and take your brochure. If you're signing at a booth, ask book-buying parents where their kids go to school and pitch them for a school visit as you hand them a brochure.

Expect that your in-store experiences will be varied. No one goes out and bags the big one every time. Consider anything over 20 books sold as a successful signing. I always carry a box of 30 books in my trunk in case the bookseller runs out. If this happens you can whip out your personal inventory and charge in like Tarzan to the rescue. The customers are happy, you sell more books, and your host doesn't go home with mud on her face. Even a signing that doesn't appear to be successful may eventually pay off in speaking engagements, media interviews and other fruitful contacts. Carry a couple of press kits just in case. The secret is to use each event to promote future opportunities.

Finally, nurture those symbiotic relationships with children's booksellers. Join their associations, attend meetings, and volunteer for committees. I did all of the above with the Southern California Children's Bookseller's Association (SCCBA) and worked myself into a Vice President position on the board. I also attended the annual retreat of the Northern California Children's Booksellers Association (NCCBA) and conducted a workshop on authors and booksellers working together to increase book sales.

Here are contacts for several associations around the country. Most sponsor annual trade shows where you may participate. These numbers are current as of January 2000, however, positions and area codes change, so check with Caron Chapman at ABC at 800-421-1665 if the number you call is no longer valid.

Great Lakes Booksellers Association (GLBA), Jim Dana, 800-745-2460, glba@books-glbaorg

Mid-South Independent Booksellers for Children (MSIBC), Jennifer Anglin, 214-827-2234

New Atlantic Children's Independent Booksellers Association (NACIBA), Ellen Mager, 215-348-7160

Northern California Children's Booksellers Association (NCCBA), Dennis Ronberg, 415-949-3390

Northern California Independent Booksellers Association (NCIBA) Hut Landon, 415-927-3937

Southeast Booksellers Association (SEBA) Wanda Jewell, 803-252-7755

Southern California Children's Booksellers Association (SCCBA), Ane or David Miller, 562-806-6490

Upper Midwest Booksellers Association (UMBA) Susan Walker, 800-784-7522

Chapter Seven

Endangered Species
The Library Connection

Libraries were once the largest consumers of children's literature, but reduced budgets and closures in the early nineties caused publishers to rely less on public libraries for the solid sales they once produced. Although libraries are recovering from that long dry season, their book budgets have not been fully restored.

According to the American Library Association's statistics, there are 122,663 libraries in the United States. Of those, 15,946 are public libraries (up from 8,865 in 1987), and 97,976 are school libraries. Making the library connection is worth your time and energy.

Explore Your Home Territory

Call your neighborhood library and make an appointment with the children's librarian. If your book has not been ordered, offer to come by and donate a copy. Arrive with brochures, your business cards, a copy of a review, and a camera.

In Indonesia people love ceremonies. They signify that an event has importance and that a bond is being created among the participants. When you get to the library make a simple ceremony out of donating your book. Have a few photos taken with the staff. All libraries have selection policies that also apply to gift books. Ask the librarian to notify you when your book is added to the collection. When you hear from her, ask her if she minds if you send the photo to your neighborhood newspaper. Include a descriptive caption. Be sure to identify each individual by name and title.

When you meet with the children's librarian, discuss some ideas for presentations:

1. Can you read your picture book during storytelling hour?
2. If you have a slide show, is there a room to accommodate it?
3. Are there programs in which parents or teachers can participate?
4. Is there a regularly scheduled event in which you can participate?

Although some libraries have small budgets for programs, I wouldn't expect payment at my home branch. Do this one from the heart. After you've decided on a venue, discuss the possibility of book sales. The library staff cannot sell your book; however some libraries allow the author or a local bookseller to set up a table for sales. Another alternative is to notify the bookseller of the event, ask him to purchase copies, and then announce the location where your book is available at the end of your presentation.

Educators often ask children's librarians if they know of any authors who visit schools. Let the librarian know that you are available for school presentations and ask her to recommend you. Hand her some brochures, a copy of a favorable review, and your business card.

Sometimes in smaller libraries local residents can reserve the display cases. Check with the librarian. Do you have artifacts, photographs, dolls, stuffed animals, etc. that can be used to create an interesting display centered on your book?

With the right approach you can also promote your bookstore signings at libraries. Just ask for the person who approves flyers. At first, librarians rejected my requests to leave flyers. Libraries cannot promote commercial events but will display flyers affiliated with nonprofit organizations. Since I volunteer regularly with the Orangutan Foundation International (OFI), I asked the vice president if I could include the OFI name as a sponsor. I got the go-ahead. It was free advertising for the group. When I walked into the next library, I introduced myself and began my pitch by pointing to the line with the OFI name on it. "This event is free," I said. "And see—it's sponsored by the Orangutan Foundation." It was approved and displayed the same day.

Expand Your Range

After visiting your local libraries, begin contacting your regional systems. Use the American Library Directory in the reference section. Call the major systems in your area and get names and contact information for the person in charge of their children's book acquisitions. Ask your publisher to send them review copies if they have not already done so. If your book is approved, it will appear on a list seen by every branch in the system.

Next, call the Senior Children's Librarian at each branch and introduce yourself and your book. Let her know that you are available for library appearances, briefly describe your presentation, and offer to send her additional information.

Ask these questions:

1. Are there any upcoming events in which I might participate?
2. Does your library system have monthly meetings for children's librarians?
3. If so, are authors ever invited to do short presentations?
4. What will be the theme of the summer reading program? (If you can tie your book into that theme, the librarian may be interested in working with you.)
5. Do you have plans to participate in any literacy events in the community?
6. What are your plans for National Library Week?

School Libraries

The best way to contact school librarians is by attending their conferences. The American Association of School Libraries (AASL) is an affiliate of the ALA. The California School Library Association (CSLA) is a regional chapter of the AASL. Search for your regional chapter on the Internet. Web sites provide a wealth of information. Consider joining your local chapter to keep up on the news and to find out well in advance where and when conferences will take place. Then you can contact the program directors to propose presentations. You might do a workshop or participate on a panel. This will be discussed more in Chapter Nine.

If you live near a large school district, call the administrative office and ask for the person in charge of acquisitions in the Library Services Department. Ask your publisher to send her a copy of your book, or better yet, personally drop by and hand her a copy. The supervisor of Library Services is often in charge of acquisitions, and a good friend to have. She's probably a member of several literacy organizations and can help you plug into them. Bonnie O'Brian holds this position in the Los Angeles Unified School District (LAUSD). This is one of the largest districts in the nation, with about 800 schools. Here's Bonnie's address if you would like your book to be considered for LAUSD libraries. She's a friend of mine—you can tell her I sent you.

Bonnie O'Brian

Supervisor, Library Services

Acquisitions

LAUSD

1320 W. 3rd Street

Los Angeles, CA 90017

213-625-6486

In Conclusion

Children's librarians love children's books. By extension they'll probably love you too. These dynamic, hard-working child advocates are happy to meet you and their relationships are worth cultivating. If you haven't yet noticed, gone are the days of the "shushing" librarians. You don't have to whisper when you speak to them.

Don't overlook school libraries. Do you live in New York, Chicago, Atlanta, San Francisco, or some other vast urban jungle? Your book could be on the shelves of several schools in their districts.

Consider volunteering for a library event. You can also donate used books and check off the library donation box on your tax return. As children's authors, we have an important stake in keeping libraries off the endangered species list.

Chapter Eight

Make 'em Laught, Make 'em Cry, Make 'em Se_uirn
A Guide to School Visits

As ordinary children's authors, we aren't the Stephen Kings of the jungle. When we roar, we don't attract awesome advances. Sometimes I wonder if someone sneaks into our tents at night to spray us with money repellent. Yes, we write for the love of it but the rewards can be more than spiritual—they can be monetary as well. We don't have to live on grubs and tubers to pursue our passion.

Making school appearances will supplement your income as well as reward you with wonderful experiences. Many authors, including yours truly, make more money from this endeavor than from advances and royalties combined. If you like connecting with kids, you could grow to love school visits as much as I do.

Be forewarned that for most schools, bringing in children's authors is a fairly new phenomenon. In an informal survey, I asked adult audiences if an author had ever visited their schools when they were kids; only three out of more than 1,000 responded affirmatively. But for those three people, the experience had remained a vivid one. So don't be caught off-guard if you're met with surprise when you present the idea to educators and parents.

To create a dynamic school presentation, you need to think of yourself as a performer. Have fun—because if you aren't enjoying yourself, neither will your audience. However, if you would rather face a charging rhino than a live audience, you're better off at home facing your computer. Don't torture yourself. You don't have to do this. Get yourself a web site instead and use it as your major promotional tool. Take solace in the fact you aren't alone. In a national survey, people were asked to name their three top fears. They were: public speaking, death, and fire. The truth is, if you hate it— you'll probably be lousy at it. It's okay to pass go and move on to Chapter Ten where you'll learn how to promote your book on the Internet.

Reasons to make school appearances:

- You get to talk about writing.
- You meet your audience face-to-face.
- You inspire children to read.
- They'll want to read your next book.
- You expose your book to hundreds of people at a time.
- You can sell copies of your book while you're there.
- You collect royalties on any books sold.
- Your publisher will love the sales that school visits generate.
- And you get paid!

Where Do You Begin?

Begin by watching other writers. Find out who does school visits and ask if you can attend a presentation. Authors' Fairs, where schools districts bring in dozens of writers, are great opportunities to see others in action. Contact a fair organizer in your area. Call, say you're a children's author, and ask permission to attend. You can go from school to school and watch several authors perform the same day.

Make the following observations as you watch performing authors:

1. How do they relate to the audience?
2. Do they interact with the children as they come into the room?
3. What is the flow of the presentation?
4. What is the content of the presentation?
5. How does the content for grades K-2 differ from grades 3-6?
6. How long is the presentation for each grade level?
7. How does the performance differ for large and small audiences?
8. How do they get the audience to participate?
9. How do they use the microphone in a large assembly?
10. What gestures do they use?

11. What props and displays enhance their performance?

12. What kind of teacher handouts do they offer?

You can study the speakers at conferences. You aren't there to steal their thunder—you merely want to observe, adapt and improve upon what you see. You can learn as much from a bad performance as a good one. If the speaker repeatedly says "uh," "you know" and "um," you'll realize how annoying it is and strive not to make the same mistake.

If you've ever done any theater it will come in handy now. I was in every play in high school, and although I didn't aspire to the stage or screen, I discovered that I enjoyed performing for an audience. It taught me how to move on stage, project my voice, and how to make the last performance sound as fresh as the first. Consider taking an acting class. It's great training for any kind of public appearance. Some authors join Toastmasters, a public speaking support group. This avenue allows you to practice in front of an audience before you take your show on the road.

Types of Presentations

Will you be more comfortable with the intimacy of a library or classroom setting? Or do you prefer a large, lively audience in the auditorium? Your preference will help determine the type of presentation you develop. In this age of computers, video games, and special effects, a mere talking head at the podium in a large auditorium may put kids to sleep. The performance presentation works best in this setting. Visuals such as a slide presentation, theatrics, or props add to the fun. In a library or classroom setting you can get away with just talking, but it's still a good idea to use visuals to emphasize and reinforce your commentary.

Teaching Presentation

In the teaching presentation you demonstrate your writing process. One way to do this is by using your book as a model, then showing kids how they can apply your techniques to their own writing. You conduct a workshop and give them feedback on their efforts. This presentation works well in a classroom setting.

Include the following:

- How do you get your ideas?
- Where do you start?
- What are the steps?
- What makes a good title?

- What's makes a good ending?

- How do you improve on your rough draft?

- What do you do when you get writer's block?

- What do you do when you're uninspired or discouraged?

The Publication Process Presentation

Here's where you show kids how ideas are transformed into books. As soon as the ink dries on your contract, ask your publisher to save and send you physical samples of the different stages of your book (they throw some of these away after the book is published). Illustrating the stages in slides works well in a large assembly, otherwise you're better off in a library or classroom where kids can see everything up close. Kids also appreciate a guest of honor's spot around the publishing campfire. Is there anything about you, the subject of your book, or the artist that will amaze or amuse them? If it's a picture book, are there any hidden pictures in the illustrations?

Include as many of the following as possible:

- The manuscript in all its stages

- The proof galleys

- Samples of artwork (sketch, photo, slide)

- A signature (The 16-page format before it's cut)

- F & G's (a "folded and gathered" unbound copy)

- Bound galleys

- The binding

- Book jacket

Performance Presentation—This is Show Biz Folks!

If you've ever fantasized about becoming an actor, or are a bit of a ham, the performance presentation is for you. But what if you don't sing, dance, or play an instrument? Well, I don't do any of these things, yet I consider myself a performer. I tell stories, show slides, read poetry, teach the kids ape vocalizations, use props, and call kids up on stage to participate. The last performance is delivered with as much enthusiasm, animation, and fun as the first.

Do you sing, act or play an instrument? Great! Incorporate these talents into your presentation. April Halprin Wayland plays the fiddle and sings a song from her book, *It's Not My Turn to Look for Grandma!* If you're an artist, draw. Using an easel works well in the library or classroom but if you're going to draw for a large audience, consider sketching on a transparency, using an overhead projector so everyone can see. The performance presentation works particularly well with a large assembly in the auditorium.

Here's How I Do It:

In my "Follow Your Dream" slide-illustrated presentation my goal is to inspire children to have big dreams and to find the courage to follow them. My objectives are to encourage them to read and explore careers in the fields of writing and science. My ideal audience is 200-300 students in an auditorium setting. While they're getting seated I walk around the auditorium shaking hands and introducing myself. I want them to like me even before I begin.

Program flow:

- Introduction   10 minutes
- Slide presentation   20 minutes
- Audience participation   10 minutes
- Q & A   5 minutes
- Close   2 minutes

Program content:

- Storytelling
- My Mexican-Hopi heritage and how it draws me to nature
- Behind-the-scenes-peek at the creation of my book
- Amazing scientific facts
- Ape vocalizations
- My nonfiction writing process
- Careers in writing and science

Make it Memorable

Mary Ann Fraser is the author-illustrator of *Where are the Night Animals?* She draws for the children. Robin Rector Krupp uses props extensively and lets kids hold them up on stage to reinforce her main points. And most important, she extends herself to touch the hearts of her young audience. Michelle Markel, the author of *Gracias Rosa*, bakes Guatemalan banana bread and gives samples to students when she visits classrooms. The bread relates to the title character in her book.

What can you do that no one else does? I explain to kids that in order to take close-up photographs of apes, I had to first learn their language. "Would you like to learn how to greet a gorilla?" I ask. A colleague of mine visited a school a year after my presentation. As she was talking to the author coordinator, a student walked by and grunted, "Um-um-wuam, um-um-wuam." The coordinator returned the greeting. That's memorable!

I have three rules: Make 'em laugh, make 'em cry, make 'em squirm. Watching me demonstrate gorilla and orangutan calls—then learning how to do them—gets the kids laughing. When I tell them stories about poachers killing mother orangutans so they can sell their babies for pets, it makes them sad. How do I make them squirm? As a consolation for not showing up with a live orangutan, I bring along a live leech named "Bubba." Dig deep and discover something that will make you and your book unforgettable.

Speaking of memorable, if you haven't read it yet, pick up a copy of Daniel Pinkwater's, *Author's Day*. It's about an author's hilarious and disastrous day at an elementary school. Although he wrote "*The Bunny Brothers*," a huge banner proclaims him as the author of "*The Fuzzy Bunny*," and he can't convince anyone, including the librarian, otherwise!

Costuming

Robin Rector Krupp is my costuming guru. She dresses "by the book." For *Let's Go Traveling*, she painted a world map on a hat and attached a toy train to its wide brim. For *Let's Go Traveling in Mexico*, she wears giant crêpe paper flowers in her hair, a red chili pepper dress, and glittering ruby heels. For *The Moon and You*, she dons a blue-sequined beret, huge crescent moon earrings, a white gossamer dress, a black-and-white cape with moons and stars, and blue-sequined heels. I can't wait to see what she'll dream up for her new book, *"The Rainbow and You."*

When Robin walks by, people often stop her to comment on her costume. But she cautions, "Some people are intimidated by costumes, so be overtly friendly to help make them feel comfortable." She also suggests, "Once you come in costume, always come in costume, otherwise children and adults will be disappointed. And whatever you do—do it big enough for the kids in the back row to see."

Regardless of how ordinary you feel, children think you're special. Why destroy that image by showing up in a tee-shirt and jeans? Consider using your book as a theme. I found a store that imports brightly colored clothing from Indonesia because that's the homeland of orangutans; I then worked with a designer to create silver jewelry with replicas of apes and monkeys. My gorilla bracelet has a map of Africa and my orangutan necklace features a map of Borneo. When kids ask me about my jewelry, they learn about the apes and where they live.

Robin Rector Krupp "dressing by the book"

Fees

What should you charge? Most authors charge from $500 to $1,600 a day. Some well-known authors can command up to $5,000. To a degree, your experience, the number of books you've published, and geographic location determine your fee—authors on the East Coast receive higher fees than authors on the West Coast. But there are other factors to consider. Is your presentation unique? Can others do what you do— or are you one-of-a-kind? Are you fluent in Spanish, Vietnamese, Armenian or other languages in demand? Has your book just won a widely recognized award such as the Newbery or the Caldecott? Is your book selling millions like Laura Numeroff's, *"If You Give a Mouse a Cookie"?*

Okay, back to reality. Unless you're already a polished and experienced public speaker, your first few school appearances will be freebies. Call schools in your neighborhood and offer your services as a visiting author. Test your presentation on these audiences to see what works. Freebies can pay off in other ways. Offer to return to lead a teacher or parent workshop for a fee. Let the author coordinator know that you're creating some promotional material and would appreciate a letter of recommendation written on school stationery. Send out press releases and see if you can get a reporter to cover your presentation.

In the first edition of this book, I suggested charging $100 for your first few paying gigs while you continued to polish and refine your performance. But the climate has changed. More and more schools have begun inviting authors. The law of supply and demand warrants a beginning fee of $300. When you feel confident, and the compliments from students and teachers begin to flow, jump to $500 for the day. If you continue to improve your performance, content, and the quality of your curriculum material, you may increase your fee by $100 annually. Before raising my fees, I call contacts at schools who've expressed an interest but have not yet booked a date. I say, "I just wanted to let you know I'm raising my fees January 1st to give you the opportunity to book a date at the lower rate." People have actually thanked me for letting them know! Sometimes the urgency of an impending rate increase spurs them to book a date.

The Three Magic Words

Now, pay attention because I'm about to tell you the *three most important words* when negotiating a fee. This is particularly useful when you're booking an unfamiliar venue. A school may be inaugurating a new library and needs an author to speak, there may be a parent conference where you can teach a workshop, or someone may ask you to give a luncheon keynote speech. When asked about your fee and you're unsure of what to charge, simply say, *"What's your budget?"* Then shut up. Even if the phone goes dead at the other end, under no circumstances speak until after the other person breaks the silence. She who speaks last—wins. Here's an abbreviated version of an actual telephone conversation I had.

"We need a Latina writer to deliver a keynote speech at a luncheon for our parent conference. Ane Miller recommended you at Through a Child's Eyes bookstore. What do you charge?"

"What's your budget?"

(Long pause.) "Well…we don't have much money. It's only a 45-minute speech and we're having another keynote speaker at dinner. We can pay each speaker $1,000."

"I can work with that."

"Great!"

When she first asked, the figure that popped into my head was $500, based on my presumption that they probably didn't have much of a budget. But did I lay my cards on the table? NO! I said the three magic words, *"What's your budget,"* and earned double the fee I'd hoped for.

Free Events

From time to time you will be asked to participate in an event for free. Schools have Career Days, nonprofit organizations hold fund-raisers, and service clubs need speakers for meetings. You must use your own discretion. When an inner city school librarian called and asked me to give a 10-minute inspirational speech at the dedication of the new library, I accepted. When a parent from a Beverly Hills school called claiming she had no budget, and asked me to teach a free workshop, I declined.

Sometimes a school representative will call and say, "My school is in a poor area and we have no money to pay you. Will you come and speak to our students for free?"

The truth is, the poorest schools have the most money because they have access to state and federal funds. The caller isn't being deceitful, she just isn't knowledgeable about school budgetary matters. It's your job to help her locate funding by asking if her school has access to Title I, Goals 2000, School Improvement Plan (SIP), or PTA funds. I've had school visits funded through all of these programs. If she calls back and says the budget for the current year has already been allocated, offer to book and event for the following year.

Whenever I feel uncomfortable accepting a nonpaying engagement, I simply explain to the caller, "I do a limited number of free events each year, and I'm booked up for the next three years."

Promotional Material

Your promotional material must reflect your fee. You can't send an author coordinator a poorly copied flyer on cheap paper and expect to get paid $500+ for an appearance. Higher fees demand professional material. You'll be providing this material to principals, librarians, PTA and school board members, cultural councils, and anyone else who expresses interest in booking you for an appearance. Your press kit easily converts into a school presentation kit. Simply replace the book jacket on the front of the portfolio with a computer-generated label that says, "Meet the Author" or "School Presentations by," then include your name and the title of your book. Omit the press release. Since I purchase my headshots in quantity, I prefer to include one so that it can be used to promote my visit when they hire me. I call this package a "press kit" regardless of whom I send it to because it's a familiar term.

Your press kit should include:

- Copy of the publisher's catalog ad
- Book reviews
- Brochure
- Letter of recommendation
- Content sheets

- Fee schedule
- Business card

Making the Connection

I know of a couple of children's authors who have been successful at cold calling schools. But, since I lasted just two days in a telemarketing job before I went bananas, I don't think I'm qualified to give you advice on how to go about making these calls, if you choose to. However, if you have the heart of a lion and the nerves of a Tasmanian devil, you can obtain telephone numbers for every school in your state by contacting its Department of Education. If you live in California contact:

California Department of Education

CDE Press, Sales Office

P.O. Box 271

Sacramento, CA 95812-0271

916-445-1260

1-800-995-4099

One of my more creative promotional efforts occurred when I was invited to set up a vendor booth in San Diego at the annual Hispanic Caucus of the California School Board Association. When I offered to conduct a workshop, I was given a spot on a panel. No honorarium was involved, but I traded the vendor's booth fee for my services as a panelist. My name on the program gave me exposure to all the board members in attendance. On the second evening I attended an after-hours dance sponsored by the organizers. Some board members pulled me out onto the dance floor and taught me "The Macarena." I was later hired for multiple school appearances by two of their districts.

22 Ways to Book a School Visit

Most of the methods listed here are covered in their related chapters. Those not discussed elsewhere are explained on the following pages.

1. Do a freebie.
2. Contact an Authors' Fair organizer.
3. Befriend booksellers and ask them to recommend you.
4. Pass out your brochure at book signings.
5. Ask author coordinators who hire you to spread the word.
6. Mention your availability in a media interview.

7. Join a bookseller's organization.

8. Befriend a children's librarian and ask her to recommend you.

9. Pass out your brochure at conferences.

10. Volunteer to speak at a conference.

11. Get on your reading council's list of speakers.

12. Participate in a showcase.

13. Advertise in a directory.

14. Set up a vendor's booth at a literary event.

15. Set up a web site, and then advertise it.

16. Offer to speak to a community group.

17. Pass out your business card at a related fund-raiser.

18. Participate in a book fair.

19. Teach a class.

20. Advertise on a group site on the Internet.

21. Say, "I'd love to come to your school," to every educator you ever meet.

22. Ask members of your critique group for referrals and return the favor.

Authors' Fairs

An Authors' Fair is an annual event hosted by a school district that invites a number of children's authors to visit each of its participating schools. This can involve as few as 10 authors or as many as 100. The downside is they generally pay around $150. The upside is that an Authors' Fair is a great place to get exposure and experience if you're newly published. Authors' Fairs may be a Southern California phenomenon. I've asked colleagues across the country and they aren't familiar with them. But, if you live in the Los Angeles or Orange County area and want to contact the "Joany Appleseed" of Authors' Fairs, she runs about a half dozen of them and is always looking for new authors, here's her contact information.

Joan Hansen

15312 Notre Dame Street

Westminster, CA 92683

714-892-3995

Showcases

Showcases are events where performers are invited to preview their presentations for buyers such as PTA program coordinators, librarians, or cultural arts council members. Singers, dance troupes, magicians, storytellers, and actors are the primary participants. Very few children's authors promote their services through showcases. Until now, it has been a well-kept secret. In order to participate, you must apply and be accepted. Sometimes a video of your performance is requested for review. When accepted, your name and a description of your presentation are listed in a catalog. A listing does not guarantee that schools will hire you. Check around for a showcase in your area. Cultural councils sometimes organize them. If you live in Southern California contact:

Program Preview Days
Chris Webb
P.O. Box 1470
Sunset Beach, CA 90742-1470
562-592-2017

Directories

The School Assembly Directory goes out to school administrators, assembly coordinators, PTA program coordinators, and over 3,500 Southern California public and private elementary schools. For $350 you get an 8½" x 11" full-page, black-and-white ad. The first year I advertised, I got no bookings. Zip. Nada. The second year I got four bookings, and the third year I got six. The consistency of my ad helped establish my credibility. This publication continues to pay off for me. The great thing is, I'm the only author! (Foolish me to even tell you about it.) The other performers do magic tricks, sing, show live reptiles, and even impersonate Abe Lincoln. I stand out from the crowd. Your ad includes a free web page on the Learning Adventures web site. This company also distributes 1,000 directories targeted at PTA members at the California PTA Convention. If you're interested in performing in Southern California, the directories are distributed annually. Contact:

Learning Adventures
5272 Thorn Tree Lane
Irvine, CA 92612-2346
(714) 786-4484, Fax: (714) 786-9383
Web site: www.theschoolassemblydirectory.com

There are several children's author directories on the 'Net. Leap forward to Chapter Ten for their web site addresses.

Adult Workshops

Although the focus of this chapter is on presentations for students, I'd like to mention the value of developing workshops for teachers and parents. Your impact on students will be even greater if teachers and parents are given the opportunity to work with you as well. This will help create an adult support system for kids that will continue long after your event is over. Another benefit is that, unlike students, adults arrive at workshops with checkbooks and many of them will buy your book.

Staff Development

By now, many teachers have had some training in the writing process. My "How to Create a Photo-Illustrated Book" workshop drew a big yawn until I restructured and renamed it, "Secrets of a Photo-Journalist." I asked schools to provide disposable cameras for each teacher, switched the emphasis to photography, adapted my handouts, and added a photo-taking session. I was no longer teaching "the writing process," I was sharing my insider trade secrets. During the photo session at the debut of my new workshop, one teacher went outside and posed for his colleagues by hanging from a tree like an orangutan. One office worker ran down the hall laughing, "Teachers with cameras are dangerous!" Everybody loved it.

Are you an expert in another field of interest to educators? My heritage is Mexican and Hopi. I teach a field study staff development course about Mexican American Culture to help educators better understand their students. So, for three solid days I have a captive audience. Of course, I end the class with a pitch for my school presentations.

One last note—educators expect supportive and practical handouts such as workshop highlights or activity sheets for classroom use. Produce quality handouts if you plan on doing staff development. I've included a few of mine in the following pages. *Tip:* Photocopy your overheads and use them as handouts.

Parent Workshops

Recently schools have been making aggressive efforts to include parents in their children's education. As an author, you can help demystify the writing process and remove some of the barriers that prevent parents from helping their children effectively. They also need to realize how important it is to simply read with their kids. You can also help them understand the value of sharing their family history and other stories so their

Page Layout & Design

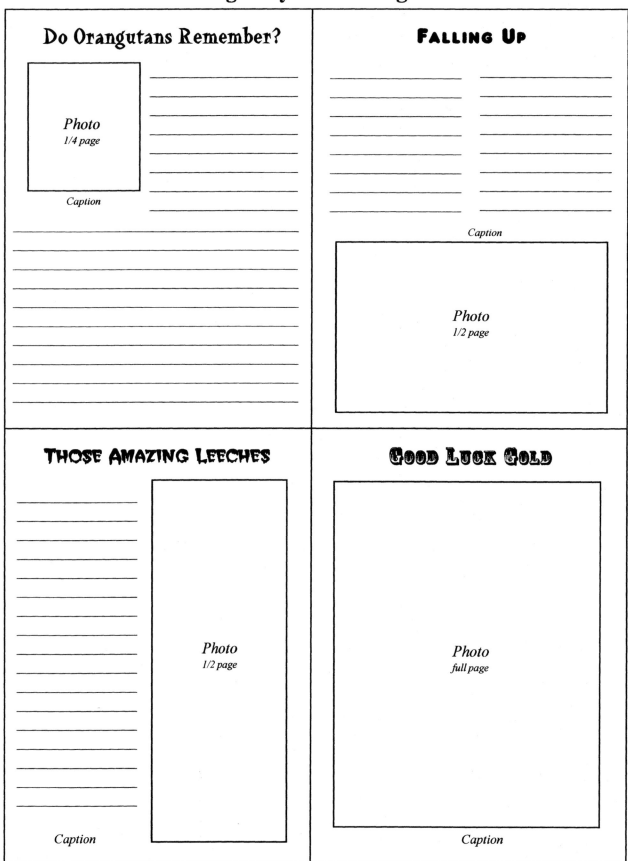

Do Orangutans Remember?

Photo
1/4 page

Caption

FALLING UP

Caption

Photo
1/2 page

THOSE AMAZING LEECHES

Photo
1/2 page

Caption

Good Luck Gold

Photo
full page

Caption

Ape Quiz

1. What is the main difference between a monkey and an ape?

2. Can you name the four great apes?

3. Where do orangutans live?

4. According to scientists, which great ape is humankind's closest living relative?

5. What is an orangutan's favorite food?

6. Do orangutans live in groups?

7. What special sounds to orangutans make?

8. What are primates?

9. From which country did Evelyn Gallardo recently return?

10. How did Mrs. Gallardo become so interested in apes?

Answers to Ape Quiz
by Evelyn Gallardo
Web Site: www.evegallardo.com

1. Monkeys have tails, apes don't.

2. Chimpanzees, gorillas, orangutans and bonobos (aka pygmy chimpanzees).

3. On the islands of Borneo and Sumatra in Indonesia.

4. The chimpanzee.

5. Fruit.

6. No. Females stay with their young for about 7-8 years. Males are nomadic.

7. The "kiss-squeak" is an aggressive, warning call ("kiss-kiss-hmm, kiss-kiss-hmm"). Only males use the "long call" to warn other males to stay away ("Ungh-ungh-ungh-ungh-ungh-roar-r-r!").

8. Humans, monkeys and apes. (Also lemurs and tarsiers.)

9. Uganda.

10. It started when she saw the movie "King Kong." She believed gorillas were really gentle and misunderstood.

kids can use this information to create authentic and meaningful writing. I offer two workshops for parents, "8 Ways to Motivate Your Child to Read and Write," and "How to Help Your Child Create a Photo-Illustrated Book." In both workshops, I show parents a portion of the slideshow their kids have seen during my assembly. This opens up a dialogue between parent and child. It also makes my slideshow pull double-duty.

Follow-up & Evaluation

After your school presentation, send a thank-you note to the principal and the author coordinator. This is particularly important when you are starting out because you want to build goodwill that will lead to word-of-mouth recommendations. Include an evaluation sheet for feedback on your performance. An evaluation is one effective way to discover where your presentation is on track and where it needs improvement. Keep it to one page. An open-ended evaluation seems to elicit the most productive feedback. *Loud Emily* author Alexis O'Neill developed this one. You can adapt it to your own needs.

EVALUATION

Date:

Author's Name:

Name of Presentation:

On a scale of 1-10 with 10 being the highest, please rate the workshop listed above.

Poor   **Excellent**

1   2   3   4   5   6   7   8   9   10

The session (circle one)

a) Met my expectations   b) Did not meet my expectations   c) Exceeded my expectations.

What did you like about this session? What did you gain that you think you might be able to apply in the classroom?

What suggestions do you have for improving this session?

I teach grade(s) _____ School_____ City/Town _____ Zip _____

Subject: _____ Name (Optional) _____

In Conclusion

It takes time and effort to develop a polished performance, to build credibility, and to become known as a speaker. I've built a reputation by always delivering more than I promise—and I promise a lot! The author coordinator knows I'm going to teach the kids ape vocalizations and show slides. What surprises her is when I walk through the audience and shake hands with her students, or when I insist on meeting each child who's purchased a book so I can write something special in it. And she definitely doesn't expect me to bring a jar of live, squirming leeches! I deliver each performance as if it comes with a 100% money-back guarantee.

Speaking of guarantees, as with any enterprise, when you're in business for yourself, expect that your income will fluctuate. Nonetheless, some authors make $25,000+ a year in school appearances alone. I made $30,000 in 1999. This is a win-win situation. The kids win because they get to meet an author and receive inside tips to help them with their own writing. You win because you get to be your own boss, you can talk about what you love to do, you promote your book, and you collect some priceless moments along the way.

Once as I was signing autographs in an auditorium, a boy standing in line clutched my book and called out, "Mrs. Gallardo, I'm going to read every book you ever write!"

On another occasion, a girl walked up, leaned close and whispered with determination, "When I grow up I'm going to Africa too."

"I know you will," I replied. "If we ever bump into to each other in a remote rain forest, come up, tap me on the shoulder and remind about today. I'll remember you."

A student once asked me, "Are you the *arthur?*" When I said yes, he faked a swoon and slid from his chair onto the auditorium floor. The friend sitting next to him picked up on the cue and followed suit. It made me feel like a rock star.

Sometimes precocious kids will ask your age, or request your phone number, a free book or even something you're wearing. But by far, my most unusual request came from a fourth-grader, who asked, "Mrs. Gallardo, can I shave your name in my scalp?"

81

Chapter Nine

Out on Limb
Networking at Conferences

If you aren't a fan of heights, swinging through the canopy can be terrifying. Your knees go weak, you're exposed to the elements, and you're definitely out on a limb.

Standing at the entrance of your first Book Expo America (BEA) or American Library Association (ALA) conference can be breathtaking. Row upon row of booths, displays, blinking computer screens, and masses of people might seem as about as inviting as a leech-infested swamp.

So why should you attend a conference? First, conferences allow you to expose your book to thousands of professionals in one location. Second, it's impossible to visit every bookstore, library, and school in the nation—and in this arena—they all come to you. Finally, the friends you make at conferences will often hire you down the line. Two years ago I met a Vice Principal from an elementary school at the Edward James Olmos Latino Book Festival in Los Angeles where I had set up a vendor's booth. Virginia Rascon and I had an animated conversation about inspiring children to read. She took my press kit and promised to invite me to her school in Yuma, AZ. It took two years to get the funding, but I finally made it to Yuma where I spent an incredibly rewarding day with Virginia's students and staff. Photography has taught me patience. I once searched the Borneo rain forest for eight days without sighting one orangutan. But on the ninth day I took the most fantastic photographs of my career. Networking at conferences is often like that. You have to be patient, persistent, and have faith that your efforts will pay off down the road.

Many organizations host regional and national conferences. When you learn of one coming to your area, contact the organizers for information. They often have web sites with online registration.

Advantages of attending a conference:

1. Thousands of people who read, write, buy and sell books are in attendance.
2. Personal contact is more effective than calling on the telephone.
3. You have multiple opportunities to talk about your book.
4. Your promotional material gets into decision-makers' hands.
5. You can promote your services.
6. You learn about the industry.
7. Your book gets wider geographic exposure.
8. People who attend literary conferences love meeting authors.

Networking Tips

Never underestimate the power of personal contact. Don't be afraid to speak first. If you show a bit of genuine interest in people, they'll be more likely to read your book, tell their friends about meeting you, or introduce you to their colleagues at the conference. Dressing up in your "author" costume and smiling a lot will help attract book-lovers. Everyone notices Robin Rector Krupp when she walks by in her sequined beret.

If you're shy about meeting new people like I used to be, stretch your imagination. What can you do to attract people? The simplest thing you can do is walk around the conference holding your book with the cover side out. Wear something eye-catching related to your book. Give people a reason to approach you. People often stop me to comment on my primate jewelry. This gives me the perfect lead-in to talk about my book and to extend a personal invitation to my workshop if I'm teaching one, or to my booth if I've set one up. I'm much more relaxed talking to someone new when they've initiated the conversation.

Exchange business cards with people you meet and add them to your mailing list. Write a note on the back of each card with the conference name and date, a few words to remind you of the conversation, and any follow-up required. Don't rely on your memory!

Although I hand out brochures to most everyone, people at conferences are so inundated with material that I suspect mine often get lost in the shuffle. I offer to mail my press kit to the people who seem the most enthusiastic about booking me.

Survival Gear

Before you head out for any conference you'll want to be prepared. In a swarm of people, you'll need to offer something tangible and imaginative to stand out from the crowd.

The Tools:

- Business cards
- Brochures
- Book jackets
- A smile
- A firm handshake
- Plenty of enthusiasm
- 10-20 press kits

The Organizations

ABA, ABC, ALA, CATE, CRA, CSLA, IRA, NABE, NSBA, SCCBA. What do all of these acronyms mean? I've listed some national organizations of interest to authors, as well as some California chapters. For complete descriptions and contact information, do a search on the Internet or check the reference desk of your local library.

National Organizations

ABA	American Booksellers Association
ABC	Association of Booksellers for Children
ALA	American Library Association
BEA	Book Expo America
GATE	Gifted and Talented Education
IRA	International Reading Association
NABE	National Association of Bilingual Education
NAEYC	National Association of Education of Young Children
NAESP	National Association of Elementary School Principals
NEA	National Education Association
NCTE	National Council of Teachers of English
NSBA	National School Board Association
SCBWI	Society of Children's Book Writers & Illustrators

State and Regional Level Organizations

ACSA	Association of California School Administrators
CADA	California Association of Directors of Activities
CATE	California Association of Teachers of English
CLA	California Library Association
CRA	California Reading Association
CSLA	California School Library Association
CSTA	California Science Teachers Association
NCCBA	Northern California Children's Booksellers Association
SCCBA	Southern California Children's Booksellers Association

The Press Room

Most conferences have a press room. Drop by a couple of times each day, stroll in like you belong there, and strategically place a few brochures and book covers around the room so they don't get buried under a pile of other materials. Don't leave too many at once—periodically the room is cleared and they'll end up in the trash. Pour yourself a cup of coffee and strike up a conversation with reporters. When you establish rapport with someone, offer a copy of your press kit. I may be breaking new ground here, but someone has to hack new trails through the jungle. Besides, no one has ever kicked me out of a press room.

Speaking Opportunities

Speakers, workshop leaders, and panelists are often booked 8-10 months in advance. Call the organization's program director, briefly introduce yourself, and then request a proposal form for speakers. It's appropriate to ask about the theme and if there are any specific needs that you might be able to fill. Also request a program from the previous event. Look it over for content and style before you write your proposal.

At most conferences, people arrive late and leave early. If your proposal is accepted, request a mid-conference time slot. Mid-morning or early afternoon sessions generally draw good attendance. This will also give you time to meet people and invite them to your event. Don't assume that you'll automatically reel in a crowd; consider it your job as a speaker to fill the room. Prepare handouts for your audience—they'll be expecting them. Handouts can include a list of your important points, recommended reading, activity sheets, or supporting articles.

Most literary conferences pay their keynote speakers, and some may offer honoraria to author-speakers, but don't be surprised if others pay nothing at all. Most offer free admission and access to exhibits and workshops. This is not always the case, however, so check the proposal form to see if you must pay your own way.

Advantages to Speaking at a Conference:

1. You'll gain exposure and prestige just by being listed in the program.
2. You'll address an audience specifically interested in your topic.
3. You can distribute promotional material at your presentation.
4. You can build a mailing list from people attending your event.
5. You may be able to trade a vendor's booth for your services.
6. You may be scouted by other organizations to speak at their events.

Book Signings

In order to sign books at a conference, you need to make your calls months in advance when publishers, booksellers, and other vendors are setting up their schedules. They need time to prepare posters and other promotional material. Call your own publisher first to find out if the company will be setting up a booth. If so, offer to sign your book. If not, make your own opportunities by calling and arranging book signings with participating vendors. Check the Internet to see if the organization that is hosting the conference has a web site. You may be able to download the list of vendors. You may also call the conference exhibit coordinator, explain that you're an author who wants to set up a book signing, and request the list.

Attend Workshops

Attend a workshop that is related to your book. People with common interests have a basis for rapport. When the speaker asks for questions or comments at the conclusion of his presentation, use this as an opportunity to network. After an educator workshop on incorporating trade books into the science curriculum, I said, "If people are interested in role models for girls, I've written a biography about a woman scientist. I'll be teaching a workshop at 2:00 P.M. in the Embassy Room. A free teacher's guide will be available and I'll be happy to answer any of your questions." Have brochures and cards on hand to give to people who approach you after your announcement.

Vendor Booths

Depending upon the conference, vendor booths can range from $100 to well above $1,000. I've traded my speaking services for a vendor's table at a few events. Broach this subject with the program coordinator after your proposal is accepted. It won't hurt to try.

Setting up a vendor booth will provide you with opportunities but no guarantees. At the very least you gain exposure and can pass out promotional material to the people who drop by. It often means returning to the same event year after year to establish credibility. Weigh the cost against the probable outcome. Consider sharing a booth and expenses with other authors. If you decide to participate, set up the best display your budget will allow. Offering freebies such as candy, bookmarks, or Teacher Guides at an educator conference will attract people to your booth.

Consider these items for display:
- Banner
- Poster
- Easel
- Acrylic brochure holder
- Acrylic business card holder
- Tablecloth
- Bookstand

After Hours

Keep your ears peeled for unadvertised after-hour events. The best contacts are often made in the relaxed atmosphere of a party. During the conference, ask people with whom you establish a rapport if they are aware of any happenings. Sometimes they'll be gracious enough to invite you.

In Conclusion

Working a conference takes time, energy and planning, but the contacts and friendships you develop will have long-term benefits. It also takes patience. You aren't selling cotton candy. It may take a year or more for the seeds you plant to bear fruit. But once you've worked a conference, it gets easier the following year. You will already have a mini-network from which to build. You're running a business, and building a business means building relationships. Many a wonderful book has died on the vine because its author wasn't willing to step outside her comfort zone and promote it. I think your book is worth the effort. Don't you?

Chapter Ten

Around the World in 80 Seconds
Going Global on the Internet

If you stampeded out of the chapter on school visits like an elephant in a forest fire, or if you would rather be burned alive than get behind a podium at a conference—this chapter is especially for you. If you set up a web site, a simple click of the mouse can deliver millions of people around the world to your cyberspace doorstep within seconds to learn about you and your book. You never have to face a live audience if you choose not to.

In the first edition of *How to Promote Your Children's Book,* the Internet barely rated a footnote in the chapter on special promotions. Very few authors had web sites in 1997—I certainly didn't. But the World Wide Web has exploded since then and the subject warrants its own chapter. Now, many authors have web sites. If they don't, they're thinking of getting one, or are in the process of designing one. If you don't have a web site yet, it's time to leave our primate ancestors behind. Let them continue to swing from the trees—while you march on through cyberspace.

But before we begin our exploration, allow me to offer a caveat here—I am by no means a techno-whiz. Remember, I'm the one who was dragged kicking and screaming into the world of computers. That's why there's such great hope for even the most reluctant writer. If you came here to learn HTML or how to build your own web site, honey, you have definitely come to the wrong person. Yes, I have a web site, but Ted Pedersen, the author of *Internet for Kids,* built it for me. He had no book promotion experience, and I had no time or desire to learn how to build my own site. We bartered services. So, this chapter is not about software, hardware, or any other technical stuff. . I simply want to show you the advantages of having your own web site, give you a few ideas on how to make your site informative and appealing, provide helpful tools so you can navigate your way through cyberspace, and share some resources that will help you promote your book and services on the 'Net.

Who Needs a Web Site?

Imagine every school online. Teachers across the nation are asking their students to write a report about an author. The one copy of your book in the school library has already been checked out. Students sit poised at their computers and do a search on children's authors. Hundreds of authors and their web sites pop up on the screen—but not yours. The Internet is no longer the wave of the future. This *is* the future. People are buying, selling, chatting, playing, reading, bidding, and doing just about everything else imaginable online. The truth is every author needs a web site.

What Does a Web Site Do?

It economically advertises your book. Imagine taking out an ad in a literary publication and you'll see my point. Magazine ads can cost thousands of dollars for a one-time shot. Your web page costs only a few dollars a month to maintain. Your site can educate, entertain, or sell your book and services. I advertise my availability for school visits, and have links to my publisher and Amazon.com for book purchases. I market this book on the Web. It's difficult to create a site that does all of the above, and you probably shouldn't try. Decide what you want your site to accomplish and focus on building your site around that concept.

Author Aaron Shepard says, "My web page's purpose is only partly to promote my books. Its other function is to get previously printed and unprinted materials to a worldwide audience. It's a partial remedy for the frustrations most children's authors feel." Aaron's service-oriented site gets thousands of hits a week.

Many authors say that educators often express appreciation for their sites as a resource and have used them to prepare students for school visits. When I get booked at a school, I always encourage the author coordinator to stop by my site for a visit, then share the address with students and staff. During presentations, I prominently feature my web site address on a display table and suggest the students visit after I leave. As for seeing tangible results, I booked several visits from my web site last year, including trips to Chicago, San Jose, and Yuma.

How do you Design a Web Site?

Several servers such as America Online (AOL) offer free web pages. Free is great. The only drawback I see is that your web site address is longer because it contains the server's name, and some servers provide impersonal addresses, making it more difficult to locate. Web design has become an industry of its own. A search on the 'Net will produce tons of web designers. There are several programs that claim that creating your own site is a snap (I'm skeptical). One of my friends hired a student from a local college to design and build her site. Another author I know jumped at the chance when a neighbor entering the industry offered to build her site at no cost. Just be aware that when someone offers a freebie, it will probably take longer than you anticipate—that's usually the trade-off. And then, if you're like me and would rather undergo a root canal rather than build your own site, think of someone you know who's a whiz at it and wrack your brain for something you can barter.

I designed my site on paper and then turned the text and concept over to Ted. I suggest spending time on the 'Net visiting as many author sites as possible. What do you like about each one? What don't you like? What can you improve upon? Then decide what you want your site to look like and what you want to say. Type up the text, scan any photos you want to use, and then compose a rough draft. If someone else builds your site for you, they'll need these basic components. If you decide to build it yourself, more power to you.

Carol Purdy is the host of School Author Visits, an online author directory. She reviews every author's site carefully before deciding to include it. Carol suggests, "The most appealing author web site has lots of color, quick-loading graphics, text that's easy to read, and is organized in such a way that it invites one to explore."

Author Sites to Visit

I'll give you a jump-start by recommending a few author sites to visit before you put pencil to paper. I've included each author's welcome message as it appears on his or her homepage to help spark your own ideas.

Aaron Shepard - www.aaronshep.com. Welcome! On this page you'll find loads of treats and resources for teachers, librarians, storytellers, children's writers, parents, and young people—all from award-winning children's author Aaron Shepard. You'll also find info on Aaron, his books, and his author visits. Invite Aaron to your school, library, conference, or special event.

Janet S. Wong – www.janetwong.com. Welcome! Thank you for visiting my Web site. Here you can get "the inside scoop" on each of my books, and hear me read my stories and poems. You can learn about my approach to poetry – how I use props to make it fun – and find out about my school visits and performances. Enjoy!

Bruce Balan – www.cyber.kdz.com/balan. Sorry you missed me. I'm out of my office right now but make yourself at home. I thought you might be dropping by so I left a few surprises for you. If you happened here by mistake you're probably wondering where you are. This is my office. I'm a children's book writer and this is where I write. Look around. Or should I say, *click* around. Have fun.

Evelyn Gallardo – www.evegallardo.com. Hello and welcome to my home page! I've just returned from Costa Rica where I was photographing howler monkeys, sloths, and volcanoes. Hang around and browse for a while and get to know me. Please bookmark this site and visit again as I'll be adding new photos, video, and entries to my journal.

If you're an educator, PTA member or conference program coordinator and would like to preview my presentation, please drop me an e-mail at EveGal22@aol.com for information about my new 7-minute preview video.

Places to Advertise Your Book and Web Site for Free

Whether you use your site to promote your book, obtain leads for school appearances, provide an international forum for your writing, or simply entertain, you must see that it has exposure by submitting it to search engines and author directories, and linking it to other literary-related sites. Your stationery, business card, brochure, content sheets, all other promotional material you create, and each e-mail you ever send should have your web site address prominently displayed.

Your first stop on the Internet should be your publisher's web site. Take a tour and make sure that your book is featured. Some publishers include author interviews. Most publishers have web sites, but if yours doesn't, check again in the near future because it's probably in the works.

Your next stop is Amazon Books at www.amazon.com. Click the "Books" tab at the top of the page. Scroll to the bottom of that page and click on "Author's Guide." Follow the directions to get your book listed and fill out an interview form. Your book and interview will now appear on this online bookstore's list. Please keep in mind that Amazon Books constantly updates its content. The procedure I've described may change in the future.

Another great stop is Kay Vandergrift's Children's Literature site. Kay offers published children's authors a free web page on her site if you send her a copy of your book jacket, headshot, promotional material, and written permission to post them. This is one of the best kept secrets in cyberspace. You'll be listed right along with Eve Bunting, Tomie de Paola, Judy Blume, and Jane Yolen—not bad company.

Author Directories

An author directory is a listing of authors on the Web and links to their sites. Some author directories offer free listings, other charge a fee. Keep in mind the Web is in a constant state of flux. Addresses frequently change. If you have trouble accessing a web site, simply run a name search on your favorite search engine for the new address. I like Dogpile because it searches multiple engines at the same time. There are several author directories and new ones keep cropping up. I've provided some addresses for you to investigate. Once your web page is up and running, send an e-mail to the directories of your choice, compliment their content, and ask to be included on their sites.

- Kay Vandergrift's Children's Literature - www.scils.rutgers.edu/special/kay
- WritersNet - www.writer.net
- Authors and Illustrators on the Web http://www.acs.ucalgary.ca/~dkbrown/authors.html
- School Author Visits - www.snowcrest.net/kidpower/authors
- Links2Go - www.links2go.com/topic/Children~s_Authors
- Author Illustrator Source – www.author-illustr-source.com
- The Purple Crayon – www.underdown.org

Bookseller Sites

Soon every bookstore across the country will be online. Meanwhile, visit the following bookstores in cyberspace.

- Every Picture Tells a Story – www.everypicture.com
- Through a Child's Eyes – www.throughachildseyes.com
- Storyopolis – www.storyopolis.com

Other Sites of Interest to Writers

- Inkspot - www.inkspot.com
- BookWire - www.bookwire.com
- Association of Booksellers for Children – www.abfc.com

- Society of Children's Book Writers & Illustrators (SCBWI) - www.scbwi.org

- American Booksellers Association – www.ambook.org

- Southern California Children's Booksellers Association (SCCBA) – socalkidsbooks.org

In Conclusion

Exploring the Internet is like gazing out at the millions of migrating wildebeests on the Serengeti Plains. The experience leaves you breathless. However, if like a scientist, you build upon data previously gathered by your colleagues, employ keen observation skills, and do a bit of your own onsite research—you'll begin to distinguish the leaders from the herd.

Begin working on your web site now. Believe me, before you know it, *every* author will have one. Determine your goal. Is it to inform, entertain or sell a product or a service? Who is your target market? Is it educators, librarians, parents, kids, or other writers? Audience focus will determine what your site looks like. A child-like and playful site will attract kids; an informative one with curriculum tie-ins will attract educators, etc. Establish a presence now. Before the stampede of children's authors on the Web leaves you in the dust.

Tip: make your domain name your own full name whenever possible. This makes it easier for people to find your site when they are running a search.

Chapter Eleven

Call of the Wild
Special Promotions

I've always been drawn to exotic places such as Kathmandu, Iguazu, Machu Picchu, and the Amazon. They ooze mystery and intrigue. I used to wonder if they could possibly live up to the expectations their exotic-sounding names seem to promise.

My first adventure was on the Amazon. It was not the place you'd expect to find a person who was terrified of bugs. At home when a bug entered the room, I left. No contest. I'd put on my most convincing pacifist face and send my husband in to dispose of the nasty beast. I would never hurt, much less kill, a fly. But, ah, the Amazon—the name kept calling out to me—I had to go.

There were no luxury liners on the Amazon in the '70's. Our first night on board a cargo boat, three-inch beetles began dive-bombing the deck. They streaked by, buzzing like downed helicopters—then bam—they'd hit a wall. When one of them dive-bombed into my hair, it got stuck next to my ear. Its wings flapped against my ear like a propeller as it tried to extricate itself from my tresses. The drone was deafening. I freaked out. I began jumping around the deck like a crazed grasshopper.

"Get-it-out-get-it-out-get-it-out!" I shrieked.

While I provided better-than-TV entertainment for the other passengers, my husband stood frozen with an I-don't-know-what-to-do expression on his face. My six-year-old daughter, Dawn, took a pencil out of her backpack and bravely tried to coax the beetle out, to no avail. Finally, one of the Brazilian men walked over and pulled the beetle down my thigh-length hair. My husband and daughter tried to comfort me while the

Brazilians shared a good laugh. They couldn't believe I'd made such a fuss over a silly beetle. I headed for my hammock.

Just as I was about to climb in, I sensed movement over my head. My gaze rolled slowly up to the ceiling. There were a dozen hairy, squirming spiders two feet from my face. I looked for David over on the other side of the deck. The men and women had been assigned to opposite ends of the boat, regardless of marital status. David was involved in an altercation. Although a sign on deck said the boat's capacity was 96, there were at least 150 people onboard vying for a place to sling their hammocks. Evidently one of the men wasn't happy with David's choice. I was on my own.

I suddenly had a vision of lying in my hammock asleep, with my mouth wide open. Spiders were writhing above me. One by one they began parachuting from the ceiling and landing in my mouth. It was them, or me. I took a deep breath, swallowed hard, and slowly removed one of my flip-flops. I aimed the sole of my shoe at two of the spiders, closed my eyes, and smashed the duo with three twists of the wrist. The squish-squish sound they made as they took their last breath made me double over in a dry heave. After a moment, I took another deep breath and finished the rest of the buggers off in the same methodical manner.

These two experiences were a rite of passage. I was never terrified of bugs again. I'd made peace with my phobia. I'd answered the call of the wild and survived.

Special promotions are a rite of passage for authors. This is where you can step out from behind the stereotypical author's demeanor and stir up something a bit more exotic. It's your call to the wild—your opportunity to choose the road less traveled. Again, you are limited only by your imagination. Special promotions can range from having the title of your book printed on notepads to having the cover screen-printed on the back of your jacket to creating your own national holiday. In this chapter you'll discover new territory—some charted—some not. Examine each path carefully, and then pursue the ones that appeal to you. After that, unleash the explorer lurking in your heart and let your inner compass be your guide.

Something About the Author

Gale Research publishes *Something about the Author* four times a year. It is an ongoing reference series about children's authors and illustrators. School librarians who used this book as a resource have contacted me for appearances. For more information contact:

Gale Research

27500 Drake Road

Farmington Hills, MI 48331-3535

1-800-347-GALE

www.gale.com

Awards

We touched on this in the chapter on working with your publisher. Winning an award is a great vehicle for publicizing your book for only the cost of a little postage. You can mail or fax press releases to the media announcing the honor. An award can serve as a springboard for media coverage, speaking engagements, and further recognition. Photocopy the award and include it in your press kit for enhanced prestige and credibility.

Both *Writer's Market* and *Literary Market Place* list several places where your book may be submitted for awards. The most comprehensive listing I've found is in *Children's Books Awards & Prizes,* published by the Children's Book Council. Check the reference section of your library. It's expensive to buy, somewhere in the vicinity of $75. The next edition will be available in 2001. If you want your own copy, contact:

The Children's Book Council, Inc.

568 Broadway

New York, NY 10012

(212) 966-1990

www.cbcbooks.org

Don't assume your publisher will automatically submit your book for every award for which it's eligible. Make your own list, check it against your publisher's, and then ask that your book be submitted for any new or important awards that may have been overlooked.

Chase's Annual Events

Did you know that June 2nd is **Yell "Fudge" at the Cobras in North America Day**? May 10th kicks off **National Etiquette Week**, and July 10th is **Don't Step on a Bee Day**. How can these bizarre events help promote your book?

Chase's Annual Events is a reference book used extensively by people who book talent for talk shows. It is organized by date and cross-referenced by subject matter. You can look up related subjects and send out timely press releases suggesting programming ideas featuring you and your book. Have you heard of **International Orangutan Awareness Week**? Well, neither had anyone else until I suggested it to the Orangutan Foundation International (OFI). They liked the idea and gave me the go-ahead to submit a free entry to Chase's. Yes, I said free. For the last five years the OFI has generated worldwide events to commemorate the yours-truly-inspired holiday. In England, one OFI member motorcycled across the country with a brave soul dressed in an orangutan costume. They got publicity galore and raised thousands of dollars to help save orangutans from extinction. You can actually create your own holiday—at no cost! You can find Chase's Annual Events at your library's reference desk, or order your own copy for $59.95.

> NTC Contemporary Publishing Group
>
> 4255 W. Touhy Avenue
>
> Lincolnwood, IL 60646
>
> 847-679-5500
>
> 800-323-4900
>
> e-mail: ntcpub2@aol.com

Free Books

As I mentioned earlier, always carry extra copies of your book. Keep them in the trunk of your car or bring one on board when you fly. You never know when you'll meet a school librarian, educator, or a member of the media, school board, PTA or cultural arts council. I once gave a complimentary copy of my book to a fellow passenger who turned out to be the president of a school board. He gave it to his granddaughter whose mother was a teacher and who eventually invited me to her school. When it comes to people with influence, be as generous with complimentary copies as your budget allows.

Mailings

Companies that sell mailing lists can be found in your local Yellow Pages. You can target libraries, bookstores, schools, etc. The Association of Booksellers for Children sells its list to members. The same information is available in the reference section of your local library. The education department for each state publishes directories of its schools. The *California Public School Directory* costs $19.50, and the *California Private School Directory* is $17.50. They are both available at:

> California Department of Education
>
> CDE Press, Sales Office
>
> P.O. Box 271
>
> Sacramento, CA 95812-0271
>
> 916-445-1260
>
> 800-995-4099

That said—let me be brutally honest here—I have never personally been successful with blind mailings. The only mailings that have ever gleaned even meager results for me were the ones that were preceded by telephone calls where I pre-qualified the recipients. I know a couple of authors who claim to have success with mailings, but they aren't talking. So until further notice, you're free to break new ground on this one. Just because I haven't found a way to make a mailing successful, doesn't mean you won't.

Museums

Can you tie the subject of your book in with the theme of a local museum? I've done several lectures that included book signings at the Los Angeles Museum of Natural History. Its gift store also carries my book. There are art, science, children's, and history museums, and more. Contact your museum association for locations near you.

Nonprofit Organizations

Some days it may seem as if your mailbox is erupting with pleas from nonprofit organizations. You try to stem the flow by throwing out most of the mailers unopened, but they keep on coming because there are literally thousands of such groups in existence. The bottom line here is—if you can't beat 'em—join 'em.

Nonprofit organizations are tax-exempt groups dedicated to causes such as saving endangered species, eradicating disease, promoting literacy, or protecting the welfare of children. Although all nonprofits use volunteers, many of them have paid staff as well. The first step in choosing a group to become affiliated with is to call its main office and request a copy of the annual report. If they won't send you one—take a pass. The needle on the seismograph is telling you they don't want you to know how they spend their money. If you have any kind of scruples you won't want the fruits of your efforts contributing to some CEO's $100,000+ a year salary. As you read through the annual reports, look for groups that spend the lion's share of their funds on the cause, and the lamb's share on administrative costs.

Focus your search on groups that are related to your book's topic. For example, Peggy Rathmann's *Officer Buckle and Gloria* is a picture book about a dog that makes a police officer's school presentation on safety tips suddenly popular by performing antics behind his back. The Humane Society, the ASPCA, and the police department's DARE program all come to mind. As I mentioned in the section on events, I am affiliated with OFI, whose president also happens to be the subject of the biography I wrote. I am also a member of the International Primate Protection League, (IPPL), Dian Fossey Gorilla Foundation, Jane Goodall Institute, and the Great Ape Project. Three of these organizations carry my book in their mail-order catalogs and offer it on their web sites. Aside from your mailbox, you can check your computer, the reference desk at your library, or ask friends for recommendations.

If you do enough research, you'll find a nonprofit organization to join. If you really want to get results, put in a little volunteer time. Never forget that you're in business for yourself, and building personal relationships is the foundation of good business.

I launched my school appearance career by writing proposals and obtaining small grants from OFI and the IPPL. My objectives were to make students aware of the problems facing orangutans, to get kids involved in helping save endangered primates, to get the word out that I was available for school visits, and to sell books. I used the grant money to do several school events that benefited from my free presentations. In return, students implemented creative projects that helped the red apes, and I received letters of recommendation, free press coverage, and enthusiastic word-of-mouth referrals. All my objectives were accomplished.

Advantages to volunteering for a nonprofit organization:

1. *You* define the amount of time you're willing to commit.
2. You meet people with a special interest in your book's topic.
3. You and your book gain exposure.
4. Your credibility is enhanced.
5. You can draw upon the group's resources.
6. It feels great to contribute to a good cause.

Special Events

Many nonprofits organize a variety of events including fund-raisers, conferences, walk-a-thons and lectures where you can offer to sign books and speak. The organization raises funds by purchasing your book directly from your publisher. And even though you don't get paid for participating, you can maximize your exposure by promoting your school appearances and upcoming events. Just arm yourself with plenty of business cards, brochures, and keep at least one press kit on you at all times in case the media cover the event.

Publications

Publications for nonprofit organizations can include a newsletter, gift catalog and a web site. When you become affiliated with a group, offer to write an article for their newsletter. The editor will love you. Be sure to include a line at the end of the piece that describes your accomplishments and lists the title of your book.

Many groups market their catalogs via the Internet. Surf the 'Net for additional groups related to your book's topic. E-mail them with your publisher's address and contact number, and explain why your book will be of interest to their members. If they don't have a catalog, check their list of recommended books, then suggest adding your book to their inventory. The organizations below offer or recommend *Among the Orangutans* for purchase:

- Orangutan Foundation International - www.ns.net/orangutan
- International Primate Protection League - www.ippl.org
- The Great Ape Project - www.envirolink/arrs/gap/gaphome

Advertising

Paid advertising is virgin territory for children's authors. I've waded through a few tributaries, but haven't discovered any Class V rapids to propel me to fame and fortune. I tried placing a classified ad for school presentations in the International Reading Association's newspaper, "Reading Today." The cost for one issue was $125. I got three phone calls, but no bookings.

By far, I get the most bang for my buck from my web site. I receive e-mails every week from educators who find me while surfin' the 'Net. Several of these inquiries have resulted in presentations. As I mentioned in the chapter on school visits, repeated advertising in the School Assembly Directory has paid off as well. The ad I placed in Radio-TV Interview Report netted 17 media interviews.

Advertising is an area where you will have to use your own judgment. If you see another author's advertisement in a publication, call and ask about her results. If an ad has been successful for someone else, it could work for you, too. Don't jump in without a paddle. Do your research first.

Write Great Ads
A Step-by-Step Approach
Erica Levy Klein
John Wiley & Sons, Inc.

Prizes

Consider donating an autographed copy of your book as a promotional prize on a radio show, at a conference, trade show, or fund-raiser. If you're attending the event, be sure to have brochures and business cards on hand when people approach you.

Video

A promotional video can turn into an expensive project. Yet it's an effective way to market your presentations. You might have a friend videotape your performance, or you can check the Yellow Pages for a video production house. You can hold duplication costs down to about $1.95 apiece if you have more than 100 dupes of your tapes made at a time. I buy video boxes with clear plastic sleeves and generate the covers in color on card stock on my home computer.

I've generated several school visits through my 7-minute promotional video. Last year, an educator at a school in Chicago contacted me. She had a new student with low self-esteem named Gallardo, the first ever at her school. She did a name-search on the Internet with him, and up popped my web site. The educator then sent me an e-mail requesting information about my presentations. After she received my promotional video, she invited me to her school. She'd gotten a double dose—first my web site, then the video. The material evidently was convincing.

Believe me, I realize I'm breaking new ground here. Unlike my advice regarding a web site, I'm not saying every author should produce a promotional video. I'm merely providing helpful information. If you have some extra money or a friend in the video business, this avenue may be worth exploring. The decision is up to you.

Documentation Video

This is a record of your complete performance, devoid of editing or special effects. Some showcase organizers may request this type of video before they invite you to participate.

Sampler Video

This 5-7 minute video is a compilation of your best work. It usually includes a short montage followed by one or two self-contained samples of your performance. This type of tape is sometimes requested by funding organizations and showcase organizers wanting to familiarize themselves with your work. Done well, it can serve as an impressive introduction.

Promotional Video

This format is similar to the sampler, but slicker. It may contain special effects, testimonials, voice-over narration, and historical information. It is also 5-7 minutes in length. Some consider this type of tape "hype." Of the three, it is the most expensive to produce.

If you decide to produce a video, a useful guide is "Creating an Effective Promotional Video." It's available for the cost of postage:

> California Arts Council
> 1300 I Street, Suite 930
> Sacramento, CA 95814
> (916) 322-6555
> 800-201-6201
> e-mail: cac@cwo.com
> Web site: www.cac.ca.gov

Specialty Items

Tee-shirts, buttons, balloons, mugs, tote bags, aprons, jackets, pens and caps are among the many items on which you can affix the cover or title of your book. Check your contract first for available rights. Again, obtain permission from the artist if the artwork is not your own. You can find manufacturers in your Yellow Pages under "advertising specialties."

I had the cover of my book screen-printed on the back of my favorite jeans jacket, and it never fails to draw "oohs" and "aahs." And my loyal husband wears a tee-shirt featuring the cover of my book.

Television

If you're the author of a picture book, perhaps you can get it on Reading Rainbow or Storytime. These are television programs where entire texts of picture books are read to children. Contact your publisher to see if someone has already submitted your book. If not, check the guidelines to see if your book matches the criteria. If you have a match, ask your publisher to send a copy of your book for consideration. Once, when I tuned into Storytime, I saw actor Tom Selleck reading my friend Susan Patron's book, *Five Bad Boys, Billy Que, and the Dustdobbin.* Va-va-voom!

Reading Rainbow

The prime objective of this children's television series is to help beginning readers develop a love of literature. Be sure to call ahead because they are only open to submissions at specific times. Check with your publisher, because if they want to charge a fee, television rights must be available at a reasonable cost.

Submission guidelines:

1. The targeted age group is 4-8 years.
2. Reading time must be under ten minutes.
3. Both fiction and nonfiction are considered.
4. The author may submit directly.
5. **Self-published books are not eligible.**

Lancit Media

Manager of Literary Properties

Reading Rainbow

601 W. 50th Street, 6th Floor

New York, NY 10019

(212) 977-9100

800-228-4630

www.pbs.org

Storytime

The ultimate goal of this series is to create an early passion for books that will help transform a video-dependent child into a lifelong reader. Storytime wants to make reading a "cool" thing to do.

Submission guidelines:

1. The targeted age group is 3-7 years.
2. There should be only two to three lines of text per page.
3. The book must be highly illustrated with quality work.
4. Reading time is 4-10 minutes.
5. Author submissions are accepted.

KCET/Storytime

Children's Programming

4401 Sunset Blvd.

Los Angeles, CA 90027

(323) 666-6500

Web site: www.pbs.org

Barking Deer, Laughing Hyenas and Other Oddities

On occasion, the odd opportunity comes your way. Like the barking deer of Borneo, you aren't sure what to make of it or what to do with it.

A few years ago Franklin Quest, now the Franklin Covey Company, contacted me. I had been using their product, the Franklin Daily Planner, and had complied with a request to drop them a note telling how it was working for me. The representative on the telephone wanted to know if I would grant permission to be featured in their upcoming annual report. It would be a color spread and include my photo and a copy of the aforementioned letter. I asked if the report could also include the cover of my book and a few of its photos. They agreed. I asked for extra copies of the report for my press kit. It turned out to be a beautiful two-page spread. There was no payment, as is the case with many credible testimonials, but I did receive a coupon good for a refill for my planner.

The following year, Murad, a skin care products company, contacted me and asked if I would participate in an infomercial. Their products had worked so well that I had sent them a note expressing my enthusiasm. There was no remuneration, the testimonial had to come from the heart. I appeared in the infomercial and still see my mug at odd hours on late-night TV.

My point isn't that I sold a million books as a result of these land-in-your-lap opportunities. Frankly, I have no way of measuring their impact on book sales or speaking engagements. My point is that on occasion an unforeseen opportunity for free publicity may present itself. Before you turn it down, ask yourself, *is there a way I can gain exposure for my book here?*

Zoos

If you've written a book about an exotic animal, don't overlook the zoo market. Suggest this avenue to your publisher's special markets salesperson. I've participated in several events at the L.A. Zoo, and its gift store carries my book.

My friend, Art Barnes, visited the Cleveland Zoo when he went home for the holidays and was impressed by a newly completed rain forest habitat housing the zoo's orangutans. He walked into the gift shop and when he noticed that *Among the Orangutans* was not on the shelf, he spoke to the book buyer and urged her to order my book. She promised to stock 20 copies.

In Conclusion

There are many innovative ways to promote your book. I hope the suggestions in this chapter will spark an eruption of ingenious ideas. Only the furthest reaches of your imagination limit you. You're an

Franklin Quest™

ANNUAL REPORT 1995

Evelyn Gallardo

Evelyn Gallardo is a writer, lecturer and primate enthusiast who has studied with renowned naturalists Biruté Galdikas and Dian Fossey. Evelyn is the award-winning author of *Among the Orangutans: The Biruté Galdikas Story,* a book she wrote and photographed entirely in the rain forests of Borneo. Like millions of other successful Franklin Day Planner users, Evelyn purchases refills and accessories for her planner every year to help her with her continued study of the wildlife she loves.

AMONG THE ORANGUTANS

THE BIRUTÉ GALDIKAS STORY

BY EVELYN GALLARDO

Dear Franklin Quest,

As a writer, public
speaker, photographer
and conservation volunteer,
my plate is heaped
extra high. The Franklin
Day Planner is perfect
for a person like me.
I have inner peace
for the first time
in my life. Thank You.

Regards,
Evelyn Gallardo

adventurer, an explorer, a trailblazer. Don't be afraid to try something new. The important thing to remember is to test-market your ideas. Let's be real here; any investment is substantial for a children's author, so before you go making a substantial investment try out a prototype. When I had my first piece of ape jewelry designed, people were immediately attracted. If no one had noticed, I would not have invested in more pieces.

And by the way, if you discover something wildly successful—contact me and share it. It's only fair. After all, I'm spilling my best secrets in these twelve chapters.

News Flash!

Stop the presses! I just received a home delivery. It's a plastic cup with a snap-on cover to carry your coffee in while driving. It's engraved with the title of Janet Wong's newest book, *Behind the Wheel—Poems About Driving*. It also includes the name of her publisher, Janet's name, her web site address, and one of her poems. She got her publisher to produce the promotional mug. A clever coup, girlfriend.

Chapter Twelve

Clan of the Kid's Scribes

Organizing a Business Group

Ever since our ancestors swung down from the trees, took a bipedal stance, and gazed out over the savannah, we've been gathering in clans and striving to improve our lives.

Published writers join professional groups to improve the business aspects of their lives. This is a quantum leap for right-brain creator-types who prefer the company of the muse to a left-brained bean counter. But a little action from the left can be invaluable. These business groups share information and leads that have impact on a writer's success. They calculate and analyze the cost of implementing an idea over its probable result. Each member benefits from the collective knowledge, experiences, and backgrounds of the group.

Writer comrades-in-arms share their woes. When a member announces that one of her books is going out of print, a sympathetic "No!" resonates around the room. While at home, the spouse's reaction might have been, "So? Write another one." Although this is sound advice, the group is more likely to raise issues such as how much remaining stock the author should purchase, how to check the contract for a clause reverting rights back to the author, and the possibility of an agent selling book club, paperback, or foreign rights.

Membership

But where do you find all these wonderful people willing to support your strides for success? Begin with your writing friends. Who do you know and respect who might be interested in forming a business-oriented group? Writers' conferences are great places to seek candidates. Ask questions such as, "What did you do before becoming a writer?" "What are your writing goals?" Collect business cards and jot notes on the back for future reference.

I belong to the Children's Authors Network! (CAN!), a professional forum formed at the SCBWI national conference in 1995. Most of us were friends and had known each other for several years. The group evolved out of a desire to approach writing as a business. Many of us had left careers in law, promotions, management, art direction, sales, journalism, graphic art, accounting, photography, and teaching. Diversity became our strength.

Factors to consider when forming your group are career goals, compatibility, strengths, and weaknesses. Attracting members with skills and experience that enhance the group is critical to its success. Although many of our members have extensive school visit experience, we were at a loss when educators began requesting our services for staff development. We were able to turn to Alexis O'Neill, who holds a Ph.D. in Teacher Education, for a "How-to" workshop.

It's a good idea to limit your membership so that everyone's issues can be addressed. But you don't want a group so small that it lacks energy and diversity. If you'd like help to form or join an existing group, call the SCBWI at (323) 782-1010. If you live in a remote area, consider forming an online group.

Purpose and Goals

The first thing you'll want to discuss is the group's purpose. Do members seek camaraderie, support, or advice on contracts? Expecting to have manuscripts critiqued is not within the scope of a business group. What are the goals? Do you want to earn a living as writers? Do you hope to promote your books into a second printing? Would you like to join forces and set up a web site? A good way to define these issues is to develop a questionnaire for your potential members.

Answer these questions:

How would you like to benefit from a group? _____

_____

What are your major concerns? _____

What are your suggestions for discussion topics? _____

_____

List your current projects. _____

_____

What types of promotional activities interest you? _____

_____

_____

What is your public speaking experience? _____

Are you interested in making school appearances? _____

What are your future plans? _____

The answers will provide valuable information and help determine the direction your group will take. If your group decides to develop promotional material, questions about background, published books, awards, honors, etc., should prove useful. When we originally tallied our CAN! statistics, we discovered that collectively we've written 100 books and have more than eighty years of teaching experience.

Meetings

Consider setting meeting dates and discussion topics in six-month blocks. This gives members the opportunity to plan their schedules, gather information, and formulate questions. Our CAN! group met for three hours once a month for the first year and a half. Now that we've covered our most pressing issues, we meet bimonthly. We meet at the same central location, with an occasional field trip to a site of literary interest. Members bring their calendars to each meeting because information about upcoming conferences, workshops and other events is often shared.

We've completed several projects such as developing a group brochure, writing a guide for school visits, and establishing an image with booksellers and educators. We've held informal workshops on "How to Develop a Dynamic School Presentation" and "How to Get Organized." Some of our discussion topics have included "Setting Up a Group Web Site," and "Is there a Spouse in the House?" We've also invited guest speakers such as a bookseller, sales rep, writing therapist, and an educator.

Discussion topics can include:

- Contracts
- Taxes
- Challenges with editors
- How to promote book sales
- How to book school visits
- How to improve presentations
- What to do when you can't write

- Conference strategies
- Finding a good agent
- How to develop a parent workshop
- Collective advertising
- Pros and cons of setting up a web site
- Participation in upcoming literary events
- How to handle letters from children

Aside from the assigned topics, we always make time for pressing concerns and visiting. A member may be in the middle of a contract crisis or a misunderstanding with an editor. She may have just received news that although her book is selling—it will not be reprinted. Sometimes after addressing the concern, we decide that the issue warrants a slot of its own and schedule it for a future meeting.

But our business forum isn't just about problems. It's about celebrating victories as well. A starred review in Publisher's Weekly? An invitation to speak at a prestigious conference? A spouse who finally respects the framed "Do not Disturb Writer at Work" sign on the office door? Bravo!

Communication

Communicating via e-mail is a tremendous time-saver. Information can be dispersed instantly and decisions can be reached more quickly. If some of your members aren't online, you may want to encourage them to get an e-mail address. I forwarded every Internet offer to get online I received to one of our resistant members. My persistence finally paid off. For those who don't have the equipment at home, they can get a free e-mail address at a cyber-cafe.

Taking notes at meetings is helpful. Either one person can do it or the task can be rotated. Not every member will be able to attend each meeting. Having an ongoing record of shared resources, information, and topics discussed will help the group assess how well it is fulfilling its goals and serving its members.

Because CAN! collaborates on projects that invite calls from educators, librarians, and booksellers, my home office serves as a clearing house for telephone inquiries. When people hear about us by word-of-mouth and call with general questions, I send them our group brochure and invite them to contact individual authors.

Projects

The goals of your group will determine whether or not you pursue collaborative projects. For instance, one of our CAN! goals is to inspire children to read. We decided that one effective way to do this is to visit schools and meet our potential readers. Our first project was to create a promotional brochure letting schools know that we were available. We estimated the cost, and each member contributed an equal share. We developed a mission statement, everyone submitted a 50-75-word bio and a telephone number where she could be contacted, and then we collaborated on the copy for the rest of the brochure. One member with a background in graphic arts pulled it all together on her computer. We distribute our brochure at conferences, trade shows, and children's bookstores.

But keep in mind that inviting authors into the school environment is still a new concept. Many people find it intimidating. Our next project was to create a step-by-step Author Visit Guide for school administrators, librarians, and PTA coordinators. Our objective was to make the process as stress-free and enjoyable as possible.

One of our long-term projects is to build educator awareness of CAN! as a community resource. It takes time to establish credibility and a reputation for good service. Even so, most of our members have been hired for school appearances through our brochures and the word-of-mouth buzz they generate.

CAN! members cooperate on other projects as well, combining our talents in new and innovative ways. Chinese-Korean poet Janet Wong and I, a Mexican-Hopi author-photographer, do a school presentation called "Across Cultures." Our writing genres are as diverse as our ancestry. We go into schools and help students, parents, and teachers approach cultural differences in a positive way through children's literature. "Authors Without Borders" is another collaboration. Michelle Markel, Robin Rector Krupp, and I incorporate the Spanish language into our presentations to help serve a diverse population.

In Conclusion

By nature, writing is a lonely profession. There is power in numbers. Forming a "clan" of your own can create a synergy that will add up to more than the sum of its parts. The support and experience members bring to your group will promote individual efforts and chances for success.

Then there are the equally tangible benefits of bonding, empathy, and the occasional standing ovation for a member's special coup. Where else would you find this kind of sustenance for the soul?

Phase 3

Expedition Debriefing

Success is a Journey

THE Penetrable Forest

I was recently invited to Florida to visit Seven Springs Elementary School. The school had been inviting authors for five years, and had found me through my web site. They had established a special tradition to commemorate the event—each author had a tree planted on school grounds in his or her honor. A bench was also purchased with the author's name and book title inscribed on it. A dedication ceremony was held on the day of my school visit. The choir sang like angels. They sang a song about nature that made me misty-eyed with pride, for before me sat hundreds of children who cared about the earth and all its creatures. My bench was placed under the newly planted tree in the "Author's Garden." It was a place where students would sit and enjoy reading a good book under the shade of a tree from that day forward. *My cup runneth over*, I thought.

I keep a sign on my desk that says, "Success is a Journey, Not a Destination." Promoting your book is an exhilarating journey. If you keep an open mind and take a risk now and then, you'll discover that an increase in book sales isn't the only reward you'll reap. You'll make friends, build support, increase your income, and enjoy a few thrilling surprises along the way. You'll have days when you connect with your audience in a way that will make you feel that writing for children is truly a glorious profession.

Yes, it's a jungle out there, but one filled with adventure. You're now armed with a compass and a detailed map. You'll not only survive—you'll thrive. "Ah-ah-ah-ah-ah-ah!"

"Metaphors" be with you, my friends.

Seven Springs Elementary Choir
New Port Richey, FL

Author with Seven Springs Elementary principal at bench & tree dedication
Photos courtesy of Jeanette Lurman

Index

Index

Did I Tell You I Love You Today - S+S
Fishing Day - Hyperion
Hold The Flag High - Harper Collins
Nobody Gonna Turn Me 'Round - CW press
Free At Last - ~~Subside Books~~
    Candlewick